$ 5 00

P9-DZA-552

THE

Creativity

BOOK

Eric Maisel

JEREMY P. TARCHER • PUTNAM • A MEMBER OF
PENGUIN PUTNAM INC. • NEW YORK

THE

Creativity

BOOK

A Year's Worth
of Inspiration
and Guidance

Most Tarcher/Putnam books are available at special
quantity discounts for bulk purchase for sales
promotions, premiums, fund-raising, and educational
needs. Special books or book excerpts also can be
created to fit specific needs. For details, write
Putnam Special Markets, 375 Hudson Street,
New York, NY 10014.

Jeremy P. Tarcher/Putnam
a member of
Penguin Putnam Inc.
375 Hudson Street
New York, NY 10014
www.penguinputnam.com

Copyright © 2000 by Eric Maisel

All rights reserved. This book, or parts thereof, may not
be reproduced in any form without permission.
Published simultaneously in Canada

Library of Congress Cataloging-in-Publication Data

Maisel, Eric, date.
The creativity book : a year's worth of inspiration and guidance /
Eric Maisel.
p.   cm.
ISBN 1-58542-029-8
1. Creative thinking.   2. Creative ability.   I. Title.
LB1590.5 .M25   2000   00-023548
153.3'5—dc21

Printed in the United States of America

1   3   5   7   9   10   8   6   4   2

This book is printed on acid-free paper. ♾

Book design and title page photograph by Deborah Kerner

Contents

PART 8 • *Be Ambitious* 185

PART 9 • *Be Truthful* 211

PART 10 • *Be Love* 235

For Ann, as always

Introduction

This book is designed to help you become an everyday creative person, creative in everything you do.

When you become an everyday creative person you instinctively solve problems more easily, see the world as a richer place, and enjoy life more. You get to use capabilities and skills that may be hidden under a barrel right now. If you're a writer or a would-be writer and begin to unleash your creativity, you write more deeply and more frequently. If you're a painter or a would-be painter, you paint more personally, passionately, and authentically. If you're self-employed, you see your options more quickly and make changes more fluidly. If you work in a large corporation, you become more self-directing, confident, and aware. Whatever you do, creativity helps you do it better; whatever the details of your life, you feel more alive. Creativity improves your work life and enriches your life in general.

Creativity is linked in our minds with poets, artists, inventors, and people of that sort. We think of the Edisons, Einsteins, Picassos, and Beethovens of the world as creative. But any job can be done more creatively and any life can be lived more creatively. What's required are certain changes: that you begin to think of yourself as creative, that you use your imagination and your mind more, that you become freer but also more disciplined, that you approach the world with greater passion and curiosity.

This book is designed to help you make these

changes by guiding you through an exploration of creativity's many facets. Over the next year, as you engage with this book, you'll learn some new things about silence, risks, mystery, even about love. Whether you're a painter or a human resources manager, a novelist or an information services specialist, you'll benefit greatly from thinking about these things and engaging, nurturing, and working on your creativity. In the process you'll grow a lot.

The book is divided into eighty-eight sections and is meant to be read at the pace of two sections a week for ten months, followed by two months when you devote yourself to a creative project. Each section comes with an exercise that I hope you'll try. These exercises are designed to increase your imagination, confidence, thinking skills, energy, awareness, and other aspects of the creative personality.

But in order to make the best use of these exercises, you'll need to have some particular work in mind. If you're a novelist, composer, or physicist, that work will most naturally be your current novel, symphony, or theoretical problem. If you're a would-be short-story writer or sculptor, that work will most likely be the story or sculpture you've been dreaming about starting for some time now. I hope you'll pick a creative project to work on before you begin Section 1, although you'll have additional opportunities to choose as we go along. If you find that you need some help in choosing, you might consult a previous book of mine, *Fearless Creating,* in which I discuss at length the art and practice of choosing creative projects.

If you don't have a traditional creative outlet—if you aren't a writer, painter, or inventor—you'll still need to choose a particular piece of work for this coming year. It might be creating a new home business. It might be becoming a more effective supervisor or working on some important company-related task, like introducing a new computer system. It might be learning how to create powerful presentations or better systems at work. It might also be something like beginning a novel, resuming the painting you used to do, or learning to play a musical instrument. When I talk about "your work" during this book, it will be important for you to have something in mind, so please take some time to consider this.

Your work may change as the year progresses. You may start out thinking about a project at your office and discover that you actually want to study architecture and build your own house. You may start out supposing that you're writing one kind of novel and, as you become more creative, you may discover that you want to write a very different kind of novel. You may begin by thinking only about work-related creativity and discover yourself gravitating toward different concerns, maybe related to your purpose on earth or your intimate personal relationships. I actually hope that changes of these sort do occur, because they will signal that you're becoming more creative in an everyday way.

In addition to asking you to think about your work, I'll also be asking you to go to your work space. I hope that you'll set aside a place in your home that is devoted to creativity. It could be a single wall where you put your computer desk, a beautiful print, and your favorite reading-and-writing armchair. It could be a whole room devoted to pottery, poetry, or personal business. It could just be the dining room table. Your work space doesn't need to be a locked and guarded place and you don't have to furnish it out of a decorating magazine. It's simply a place that you begin to associate with your own creative efforts.

How will you use this book? I hope in three ways. First, it's to be used as a companion to a year's worth of creative work. You will need to monitor and pursue that work in your own way, because the exercises I'll present will not lead you in a linear progression from point A to point B to point C. Each will involve you in an aspect of the creative process, each will help you grow as a creative person, but the exercises are not like instructions in a manual or steps in a plan. So, in order to write your novel, make specific changes at work, or start your own business—whatever your work for the year happens to be—you'll need to keep track of that work separately. A wise way to go about that would be to keep a special journal in which you make schedules, create to-do lists, monitor your progress, and in other ways help your work along.

Second, I'd like you to experience doing some odd, unusual, and ultimately wonderful things this year, like sketching outdoors, shredding a textbook into confetti, and cooking an omelette with the shells included. These activities may not connect directly to the creative work you've chosen to do, but they will connect fundamentally to your growth as a creative person. If you've decided that this year you'd like to make an important move at work and are using this book to help with that move, it may seem strange to walk blindfolded across a college campus or have lunch in a hospital cafeteria, which are some of the activities I'll be recommending. But each of these activities and experiences supports your move in a deep way. These odd activities amount to a creative education.

Third, and ultimately most important, I'd like

you to become an everyday creative person, creative at everything you do. So although you'll be working on a particular project this year as you read this book, you'll also be changing and growing into a fully creative individual. As the year progresses, you'll become more passionate, smarter, braver, more imaginative, even wiser and more fun-loving. Each of the book's sections and activities is valuable in this regard not only for the help it will provide in getting your project done but because it will work to incrementally transform you into an everyday artist.

As a creativity consultant, psychotherapist, and college teacher, I've learned that virtually everyone finds it hard to nurture and unleash his or her creativity. Inner noise, doubts, fears, old traumas, practical problems, and a long list of other obstacles keep most people from creating and living creatively. Because the wait to manifest their creativity becomes such a long one, doubts double and triple. People wonder if they're too late. They wonder if they have too much to learn. They wonder if they can tolerate and survive the mistakes they know they'll make. Above all, they wonder if they can really begin, having waited so long already.

These obstacles are real and significant. But people discover that they can begin. You can begin this very day to grow creative. I've been writing books for creative and performing artists for a dozen years and what I hear from readers is that my support and advice help them get their creative work done. It's feedback of this sort that has prompted me to write this new book for everyone. You can become a creative person and you don't have to slip away to a retreat off the coast of Maine to do so. Creativity is exactly the same thing as using yourself richly, right where you are, at extraordinary tasks but at very ordinary tasks also. Let that be what this next year is about: becoming a creative human being, creative at everything you do, who by the end of the year has completed some strong creative work and looks at the world through new eyes.

PART 1

Begin

Weeks 1 - 4

1. Make Creativity Your Religion

Many of us are confused about how to knit together a meaningful life. In search of ways to honor ourselves and to honor life we turn to organized religion, New Age spiritual practices, volunteer work, our job, or our child's extracurricular activities. But even people thoroughly immersed in their religion, job, or child often feel that they are lacking something or missing out on something. Creativity is a route to fulfillment that you can either add to what you're already doing or make your central religion.

Anthropologists estimate that a hundred thousand religions have appeared so far. Each provides a vision of how life should be lived. But even the religious person is troubled by the contours of modern life, which typically include twelve-hour work days, a long commute on choked highways, physical and mental exhaustion, and doubts about life's meaning. What chance does the soul have to flourish in all this rush and against this backdrop of doubt? How can a person make use of her skills and inner resources if she's running eighteen hours a day, performing one task after another? Even if she has the luxury not to run so much, what will she do with her time if she's not sure that life has any purpose? The temptation is to turn on the television or to take long naps. But these solutions do not make a person feel good. By the end of the day, the majority of us feel like we're barely surviving. Exhausted, we throw ourselves into bed for a night of fitful sleep.

I think the answer to these problems is to make creativity your religion. You can either make it an important supplement to your Catholicism, Judaism, or Buddhism, or you can make it your primary religion. Why choose creativity? First, because creating is soulful work. When a person loses herself in the creative act she suddenly participates in the mystery of life. Second, creativity allows a person to really manifest her potential. Rather than feeling unfulfilled, as so many of us do, when you create you get to use your overflowing heart, your billions of neurons, and your own two hands to make a little sketch or a wall-size mural, to think a little thought or bring a whole new theory into existence, to make a little change at work or re-vision work entirely.

> *One's religion is whatever one is most interested in.*
> — J. M. BARRIE

The Israeli painter Ari Goldman explained: "Spirituality for me is the sum total of all the acts of my day." Your new religion will need its precepts and its liturgy, but first it needs its activities. It needs to be lived. Making creativity your religion means doing, beginning with our first exercise.

EXERCISE 1A • *Write Your Autobiography*

I'd like you to write a 2500-word autobiography. Your first thoughts are probably "That's too hard" and "Why bother?" Let me answer the second question first. I've taught hundreds of adult re-entry college students; each wrote an autobiography and all were transformed in the process. Writing a 2500-word autobiography is its own kind of creative act and looking back at one's life is a revelatory experience. It can be hard work, intellectually taxing and emotionally draining, but it's invaluable work and exactly the right kind of work to inaugurate our religion.

You might be wondering what exactly you're supposed to write about. Just write your truth. Write about your family's secrets, its rules, what it felt like to have a stepfather appear, what messages you got about your worth and potential, what made you feel happy and what made you feel sad. Write it chronologically or any way you like. If you launch right into this exercise you might get it done in the next few days, but don't worry about how long it takes. Just commit to doing it.

> *Religion is everywhere.*
> *It is in the mind, in the*
> *heart, in the love you*
> *put into what you do.*
> — PIERRE AUGUSTE RENOIR

EXERCISE 1B • *Name Five Obstacles*

Name five obstacles that prevent you from realizing your creative potential. "Too little time" is pretty much a given. "I have no creative potential" is an unacceptable answer. And while it may be accurate to put down "fear" five times, please elaborate and identify what exactly you fear. That you'll make a mess? That you'll be proven a fool? That you'll be criticized? Take some time to consider what stands between you and your own creativity.

WEEK 1

2. Craft Ceremonies and Rituals

We live in an extremely ceremony-less culture. A ceremony is an event meant to acknowledge that something special is happening and to support the gravity, joy, and mystery of the moment. While we get to sing as a birthday cake is brought out or stand solemnly as the bride and groom walk down the aisle, on an average day almost nothing has this feel to it, because almost nothing on an average day feels truly special.

But our hearts tell us that we're missing something. When we hear about a parent and child reading together every night before bed, we understand that their routine is elevated to the height of ceremony by the mutual love and attention their ritual reflects. When my students finish reading to the class a private piece they've written about their alcoholic father smashing their toys at Christmas or about the rape they experienced while delivering the mail, my response is always the same: "Thank you." That "thank you" is a ceremonial acknowledgment that they've done something important in telling their story.

Art class was like a religious ceremony for me. I would wash my hands carefully before touching paper or pencils. The instruments of work were sacred objects to me.
— JOAN MIRÓ

If instead I started out by mentioning that their piece had pronoun disagreement problems or ended more weakly than it began, I might be saying an objectively true thing but I'd be ruining and trivializing the moment. It is my choice, and in my classes I choose to create a ritual to make the moment feel special. This is what you as an everyday creative person can do. You can choose to make life feel more special by crafting your own rituals.

When an everyday creative person has an interesting idea pop into her head and she stops to write it down, rather than letting it slip away, that is a small ritual acknowledging the importance of her own ideas. When a million tasks confront her and she stops to meditate and breathe for three seconds, rather than rushing on as if she had no self, that is a small ritual acknowledging the sanctity of her being. These are ceremonies and rituals that everyday creative people learn to craft and enact.

I make each day feel special by starting out creating. When I was younger, I wrote late in the day—and I wrote comparatively little. But for the last ten years I've gotten up and gone straight to the computer faithfully every morning by six, in a ritual way, and by eight or so I have my writing almost done for the day. In this way

> *I try to work every day, even when I'm not motivated. Ritual is very important to me.*
>
> — MEL RAMOS

I've written ten books in ten years. This writing time is a special time. I profit by sitting there every morning, working, trying, failing, succeeding. My biological clock has reset itself and I have switched from being a night person to a morning person. These early-morning writing sessions are just that important.

EXERCISE 2 • *Craft One Ceremony*

Please engage in the following ceremony twice a day, once in the morning and again in the evening, for the next three days running.

Purchase some tea that you like and a special mug to use for this ritual. First thing tomorrow morning, right after you brush your teeth, heat up some water for tea. During the two or three minutes that the water is heating, say to yourself, "I have always dreamed of _____." See what wells up to fill in that blank. It might be "becoming a ballerina," "writing a romance novel," "traveling to the South Seas," "becoming famous," or "being my own boss." Allow your biggest dream to fill in that space.

If it's a dream that can't be accomplished (because becoming a ballerina at forty is out of the question) or that requires only time and money (like traveling to the South Seas), laugh and say to yourself, "Next dream, please." You're looking for a big dream that's at once doable and requires that you really use your skills and talents. So try again until you arrive at something that fills that bill.

Take your cup of tea to a chair by the window and as it steeps enjoy the warmth of the cup, the tea's aroma, and the dream brewing in you. There is nothing for you to do. Just be with your dream, love it, and accept it. In the evening, as your water for tea is heating, repeat your dream: "I've always dreamed of writing a mystery." "I've always dreamed of sculpting." Do this again for two more days.

At the end of the third day, craft your own small ceremony that honors your dream and that keeps it alive. Maybe you'll want to put yourself in mind of your dream as you go to bed, so that you can be with it all night. Maybe you'll want to start a journal in which you enter thoughts only about this dream. Enact this ceremony every day for the rest of the year— and for the rest of your life.

WEEK 2

3. Make Time

In a prose piece that is one of the seminal works of existential literature, the poet Rilke describes a man who gets it into his head to calculate how many seconds he has left to live. Once he makes this calculation and begins to obsess about the relentless nature of time, which will not stop and which he can now viscerally feel passing, he experiences time in a new, horrible way. Each passing second brings him closer to his inevitable death; and since a second is too short a span in which to get anything done, he does nothing but manage to make death his constant companion.

This piece, "The Notebooks of Malte Laurids Brigge," is about the psychological experience of time, about how the mind can make of time anything it will. When we are waiting for the pot to boil or a boring meeting to end, time takes forever. Those few minutes drag on so long that we feel we could write *War and Peace* and have time left over. But at other times, when we are actually writing *War and Peace,* time flies by. We sit down, vanish in our work, look up, and two hours have passed. How can a minute of meeting time feel infinitely longer than an hour of novel-writing time?

As a therapist, I've acquired a feel for fifty minutes. It may not sound like much time, but a great deal can be accomplished in fifty minutes. In a session with a client, we could learn a great deal of importance about his childhood. We could map a detailed plan for next year that readies him to write his symphony. Fifty minutes is an extraordinary amount of time, if it is used well. This is what an everyday creative person wishes and demands at least some of her time to feel like.

Time is *the* issue, because it stands for so much. There is the matter of having too little time, because of all the time your job eats up. There is the equally profound matter of feeling too drained and brain dead to get your creative work done in the time remaining after work. Even more important is not feeling up to creating and blaming time for what is really motiva-

> *When I am working on a book or a story I write every morning as soon after the first light as possible. There is no one to disturb you and it is cold and you warm as you write.*
>
> — ERNEST HEMINGWAY

tional malaise. Time can be the enemy and time can be the scapegoat.

People who want to create and who also work a day job get up earlier than other people. They make time. People who do not want to create, even if they have luxurious amounts of time on their hands, have "no time" for their composing, writing, or painting. We can carve time out of thin air, or we can fill up even infinite stretches

> *We must use time creatively, in the knowledge that the time is always ripe to do right.*
>
> — MARTIN LUTHER KING JR.

of time with nothingness. These are our choices. You can make a quarter hour appear from nowhere if that's really your heart's desire; wanting it to appear is proof that you're becoming an everyday creative person.

EXERCISE 3 • *Make an Hour*

If you don't have one already, buy a kitchen timer, one of those wind-up timers that can go for up to an hour, that click loudly as they wind down, and that "bing" when the designated time is up.

Wind it up and put it next to you. Sit. You will find the experience intolerable because of the loud ticking. This is how it feels to become too conscious of seconds. Now put the kitchen timer in another room, one close enough that you can hear the ultimate "bing" but not so close that you can hear the moment-to-moment ticking.

Today, set the timer for twenty minutes. Do absolutely nothing. Twiddle your thumbs. Do not read a magazine. Do not start the laundry. Do not just grow restless. What a long time twenty minutes can be! Wait for the blessed "bing." Then get on with your life.

Tomorrow, set the timer for forty minutes. Sit. Stare into space. Again do nothing. Don't meditate.

No yoga. Do absolutely nothing. Aren't forty minutes an eternity?

The day after tomorrow, set the timer for an hour. But this time do not do nothing. Do something. If you have a creative project in mind, work on that. If you haven't chosen a creative project yet, spend the hour engaged with your possibilities. Sketch the house you might build. Start a plan for your home business. Outline your book. Get acquainted with your dreams.

Wasn't that a different, better experience?

An hour is an incredible amount of time, incredibly oppressive if you're avoiding your chosen work, incredibly spacious if you're using yourself well. One of your jobs for the coming year is to make at least one good hour magically appear every single day, as early each day as possible.

WEEK 2

4. Make Space

A person learning to unleash his creativity often discovers that his customary space, no matter how large or well-furnished it is, must, since it was never set up to support his creativity, be re-envisioned and rearranged.

Maybe the room you call the dining room needs to become your dark room. Will that seem strange to visitors? Not if you smile and say, "Come, let's eat in the living room." Maybe your country kitchen, with its easy water supply and ceramic tile floor, is the right room for your pottery work. Will your children complain that you're embarrassing them? Not if you seriously say, "I have it in my heart to pot, and you don't want me to die of a broken heart, do you?"

Maybe the guest room needs to become a library/
study, full of your newly acquired books on the cui-
sine of the Middle Ages and your notes for your first
cookbook. Will your next guest
complain if he has to sleep on the
living room sofa? Not if you wink
and say, "Would you like blueberry pancakes for breakfast or
applesauce muffins? Or *both?*"

*It took me years to think
that I deserved a real
space. Really, I'd say
eighteen to twenty years.*
— AN ARTIST

You need this sort of space if
you're going to create. To be sure, all space is space in
which to create. An everyday creative person finds all
space sacred. You could stop anywhere in your house
and have a thought. You could sit on the floor anywhere and sketch. You could plot your novel while
doing the dishes or solve a math problem while sort-
ing the laundry. But for some activities, such as
painting or potting, a separate sanctified space is vital. In addition, the act of turning an abundant
amount of space over to your creative efforts means
that you are really making creativity your religion. By
designating a room as your writing study or rearrang-
ing the garage so that your band can practice in it,
you are setting up a sacred work space and honoring
your commitment to realize your creative potential.

EXERCISE 4 • *Make Minimum Space*

First, you need a computer desk, a computer, and
the ability to go on-line. Why? Because if you decide to learn to tango, the Internet will point you
to lessons. If you decide to design your next house,
computer software will help you visualize thousands
of possibilities. If you decide to buddy up with a friend
and support each other's nonfiction writing pursuits,
E-mail will keep you in contact. Yes, you can create

without owning a computer or going on-line. Yes, you can point to famous writers still tapping away on their Royal typewriters. But for many people, joining the computer world makes it easier to overcome obstacles to creating.

Second, you need a thinking spot separate from your computer space. This is where you read, muse, stare into space, dream, put up your feet, make notes, make plans, make sketches, travel to Spain in your mind, scratch your head, and let time stop. Pick one chair, maybe a really comfortable one with the best view in the house. Have a good-size table beside it to hold your lamp, your coffee mug, the book you're currently reading, your notepad, and your thinking pen.

A few years ago I redid my studio, which felt really good. I made it a space where I wanted to be.

— AN ARTIST

Third, you need a special bookcase. Here you'll keep the books that support your current creative endeavor. Imagine a bookcase with four shelves. Say that you're starting to write an adventure novel. On the first shelf you might collect your favorite adventure novels from childhood, which commune with you as you work. On the second shelf you might keep reference books about schooner lore, meteorology, cartography, and whatever else will provide your yarn with verisimilitude. The third shelf might be your writing altar, on which you put a handmade icon, some totems, and a nicely framed colored sketch of the cover you envision for your book. On the bottom shelf you might keep your writing resource books, the ones about agents, editors, and the publishing business.

Fourth, you need whatever other space your particular creative endeavor requires. Be generous and realistic. How much space does a pottery studio take up? Think that through. Ask the person at your pottery supply store. Buy a book on setting up a pottery studio. Start to make decisions about whether you'll need your own kiln or whether you'll find one to use elsewhere. Will you be working on a wheel or hand building? Think through what your studio will need and then make it happen.

Over the next three days—or however long it takes—pick a thinking spot, clear out a bookcase, and make the space you need for your creative efforts.

5. Invest in Erasable Boards

Organization can be a real challenge for each of us. It is even more of a challenge for everyday creative people who have lots of ideas, dreams, goals, responsibilities, and just plain things going on, and who are also a little suspicious of organization. But every creator needs a filing system and to-do lists, even if books are also stacked by the hundreds all over the place, and no pencil with a point can be found anywhere. It isn't of life-and-death importance that the house be clean or that you remember everybody's birthday, but it is vital that the chaos of ideas that start to flood your brain when you open up to your own creativity have a place to be sorted and saved. If you don't give them that chance, then chaos overwhelms you and no work can get accomplished.

Many of us feel depressed, defeated, and incapable of creating for just this reason, that the swirl of ideas inside our head keeps swirling with no place to go. But something as simple as organization can turn that around. Investing in large erasable bulletin boards is an excellent starting point. In order to weather every storm in life, you will need more than erasable boards, but those boards help enough that they amount to a fantastic investment.

> *Once you concentrate on organizing, ideas fall into place with an almost audible click.*
>
> — JANE HARRIGAN

I use four of them. Each is about three feet by four feet. I've made one into a four-month calendar. Another is for messages to myself, quotes that I like, and affirmations. The third is a to-do list having to do with the marketing of my books. On the fourth I keep track of my projects: where book proposals are, when galleys will arrive, that sort of thing. Creators may fear organization, considering it a hallmark of conformity, but maintaining these four erasable boards does nothing to stifle my innate wackiness. They are a terrific help and in no way a restriction.

A while ago I was counseling an artist couple— a painter and a writer. One week they came into a therapy session and recounted an argument they'd had about fixing a broken window. They had what seemed to me the odd idea that replacing the window should take about an hour, so trifling an amount of time that each considered the other a monster for not sparing it. I have a small erasable board in my office. I said, "Let's figure out how much time it takes to replace a window." They looked pretty skeptical about the wisdom of such an exercise, but I launched into it anyway.

We listed the steps—finding out which store sells glass, driving there during rush hour, picking the right piece of glass and putty and tools, coming back, realizing that neither had a clue what to do, starting the job anyway, somehow getting the old glass out, standing there looking at the gaping hole, botching the repair, etc.—and came up with six hours in a best-case scenario and twenty in a worst-case scenario. At the end of this foray into reality testing the writer said, "When you began, I thought this

The triumph of anything is a matter of organization.
— KURT VONNEGUT

was an idiotic exercise. But maybe neither of us looks at things too realistically."

Organize your reality. You'll feel better and do better.

EXERCISE 5 • *Invest in Erasable Boards*

Get several large erasable boards. Three is a good number. Each should be about three feet by four feet. Also get a healthy number of dry erase pens in red, blue, black, and green. You may also want an eraser and liquid erasable board cleaner. This will cost you a bit, over a hundred dollars, but it may change your life; and home office supplies of this sort are usually tax deductible.

Try out your boards in the following way. Use one as a calendar. Freehand, draw horizontal lines two or so inches apart and enough vertical lines to create the seven days of the week. This should give you between twenty and thirty weeks. Use this board to indicate your daily goals; for instance, a "1" in red for fourteen consecutive days might mean that you're hoping and intending to work on chapter 1 of your book every day for two weeks running. Use the second board for messages to yourself and for your daily affirmations. Use the third board to plan: the steps to creating your home business, the chapter-by-chapter outline of the book you're writing, the names of the books you mean to read in order to teach yourself evolutionary theory.

If you have no project in mind yet, buy the boards anyway and put them up on your walls. You'll find them irresistible: they'll draw a project right out of you.

WEEK 3

6. Settle into Mystery

Creativity is a mystery religion. An everyday creative person celebrates, honors, and lives with mystery. The mysteries of the universe can only be participated in, not solved, and when your creativity is pulled from you in the making of a song, an on-line business, a little sketch, or a large new invention, your response is not, "Well, I guess that settles the mystery of life!" Rather, it's "What a fine interlude that was, spent I-don't-know-where!"

Where is that other realm? Just in your own mind, probably. When you create you lose yourself in your own knowing and come back with an idea, a feeling, a character, a better mousetrap. Do you stay lost in your own mind that whole time or do you travel out of your body to the stars and back? I wouldn't know. Is it really your own mind at work or does a Muse visit? I don't know that either. These are real mysteries. Is the line of poetry you create brand new, born of a person who's been alive only for a tiny speck of time, or is it ancient, a product of the species' DNA and mysteries that go back to gatherings of gods or to the workings of pure mathematics? I wouldn't know. Do you? Does anyone really?

Most people hate the idea that they've been dropped into an insoluble mystery. They want answers and assurances. They want to know God's plans and how many words make a novel. They want to know which clues should be considered and which clues discarded as they search for the meaning of life. They want to know who is more right: the priest, the scientist, or the entrepreneur. But not worrying about all of that is the better

> *After all the great religions have been preached and expounded, man is still confronted with the Great Mystery.*
>
> — CHIEF LUTHER STANDING BEAR

plan. The more rewarding path, which leads, not to a final answer, but to a sense of having lived fully, is to create. In the religion of creativity, this is our cosmology myth: that when we create we make interesting worlds and fine use of our innate resources, without, however, solving life's ultimate mysteries.

Perhaps you want to make a film, compose a concerto, or unleash your creativity in the service of your study of anthropology. Maybe your goal is to be creative every day in a variety of ways: in business, with your lover, and as you make dinner. Your hope is that if you make time and space, invest in erasable boards, and are diligent, disciplined, and organized, you'll accomplish your goals. This is a good plan. But don't forget about mystery. Remember that the creative act is an adventurous whirl in the cosmos. You may enter your imagination hoping to retrieve a simple song and return with a symphony, or vice versa.

EXERCISE 6 • *Settle Into Mystery*

I would like you to write a poem. What is a poem? That's its own mystery. Please accept that there are no rules about poetry and that one word is a poem sometimes, that whole books can be poems, that objects and people can be poems, too, and that rhyme and meter are the least of it. Maybe when you write a poem you are just in a heightened or deepened state out of which flow things like lines and stanzas. Who knows? Just go ahead and write poetry, without benefit of rules, models, or a decent definition.

> *I have spent the last three nights almost entirely in the forest. You hear the owls and the frogs having a concert, and then the stags come down to drink.*
>
> — ROSA BONHEUR

Settle into mystery as you would settle into your most comfortable chair. Listen. Have visions. Let words dissolve and recrystallize and dissolve again. Travel to every continent and to all the planets simultaneously. Grow so quiet that you can hear the stoplight a mile away changing from green to yellow to red. Lose yourself; then come back with the last line of a heartbreaking eulogy, the dancing middle of a happy-go-lucky tune, or a word so full and pregnant that it gives birth right in your mind.

You may be balking. Perhaps you're saying to yourself, "What would I do with my poem when it's finished?"; "What if I have no poetry in me?"; or "What if I like my poem and start brooding about whether I should submit it for publication?" Put these thoughts aside and just participate in the mystery. Maybe you'll put two words together and change your life forever. Maybe nothing whatsoever will come of the experience. Maybe you'll paint a picture with words and exclaim, "Wow, I did good!" Maybe you'll make a horrid little mess. Can you not think about any of that and just write some poetry? Please try.

An everyday creative person participates in the

mystery. For the next three days, be that person by writing poetry.

7. Get Anxious Calmly

If you give up your salaried job in order to start your own home business, that's a creative act but also pretty scary. Suddenly there's no paycheck, but the bills haven't stopped arriving. If you give your life over to a tough mathematical problem, loving it for its intricacy but also hating it because it will not unravel, many anxious thoughts will go through your mind: can this problem be solved at all? Am I smart and lucky enough to be the one to solve it, or will it be one of those whiz kids from MIT? If no one can solve it, will I have wasted my life and my intelligence on this miserable conundrum?

When you face a blank canvas, that can make you nervous too, as you feel the pressure to create something worth an expenditure of canvas, paint, and time, something that you'll like when it's done and that doesn't scream out, "Amateurish!" Maybe you crave writing a screenplay or mastering chaos theory but feel too anxious to begin because you doubt that you have the talent or the brain power. Or it could be that you want to make your mark by presenting workshops in your field of expertise, but the thought of performing and putting yourself on the line scares you silly.

It turns out that creativity and anxiety travel the same road together. Just as the Buddhist pays special attention to suffering and the Christian pays special

attention to sin, the everyday creative person pays special attention to anxiety. She understands that she
must write her songs against a backdrop of anxiety,
and that because of anxiety she
may be tempted by tranquilizing
drugs. She understands that her
inability to write her novel and
her anxiety about writing a bad
novel are somehow intertwined, and that if she could
just calmly say yes to the book it would spill right
out. I am calm as I write this, but also anxious, anxious about getting this section right so that I do not
fall behind on my schedule and raise the specter of
missed deadlines and upset editors, calm because I've
written many books and have the sense that this section is going well. Is life nothing but suffering? No.
Are we perpetual sinners? No. Is there nothing but
anxiety? No. But there is plenty of anxiety to go
around; it is real, and it matters.

> *To be balanced is*
> *to be balancing.*
> — RAY GRIGG

Every creative person learns firsthand about anxiety. He learns that anxiety has the power to stop him
in his tracks and send him to bed with a depression.
Because he's anxious for a split second while painting,
he makes a stroke that is impulsive rather than intuitive and ruins his painting. Because he's anxious that
his not-yet-written opera will receive hoots and catcalls at its first (and last) performance, he doesn't write
it. An everyday creative person learns a lot about anxiety and, if he's willing, a lot about calmness too. He
learns, for instance, that it's possible to be anxious
and calm simultaneously.

EXERCISE 7 • *Engage in a Lifeboat Drill*

There are two kinds of calmness. One is the equivalent of sitting in the sun in a deck chair listen-

ing to the waves lapping against the side of the cruise ship. The other is noticing that the ship is going down, getting up from your chaise longue swiftly but without panic, and making your way to your assigned lifeboat station. The first is anxiety-less calmness, which we experience about as frequently as we do cruises to the Greek Isles. In the second case, anxiety is very much with us, but so is the calmness that comes with deliberate doing.

> *I'm in good form, taking no interest in things, neglecting clothes, meals, company, and feeling calm and stable as I write.*
>
> — BERTOLT BRECHT

For this exercise, find or buy a raucous bell. Once a day for the next three days engage in the following drill.

1. Ring your bell loudly and shout, "Create!"
2. Feel the anxiety well up.
3. Gather your wits and say to yourself, "I know what to do."
4. Go to your work space.
5. Set your kitchen timer for ten minutes.
6. If you're working on a book or building your home business website, boot up your computer. If you're weaving, prepare your loom. Prepare to work.
7. Work for ten minutes.
8. When the timer "bings," shout "All clear!" (If you feel like working more, please do.)

The drill is over. What you'll notice is that a bucket of adrenaline got activated just by announcing that it was time to create, but that crossing to your work place in a deliberate way and matter-of-factly working settled your nerves. The anxiety subsided and you could focus on what needed doing. Maybe you were still anxious; but you were also calm.

8. Do the Tiniest Thing

Over the years I've learned a lot about "chunking." A chunk is a manageable bit of writing, like the sections in this book, which are each about 800 words in length. I don't have an 80,000 word book to write, only a nice, easy daily chunk. I don't remind myself that I have several books with looming—and simultaneous—deadlines lined up. I don't look ahead to the revisions that'll be needed. I only think that today I have a small chunk to do. Today I have this tiny thing on my plate, this perfect appetizer.

This book is outlined and I know what each day's writing is about. But what if I were in the middle of a novel, perplexed about the plot, and not sure where to go next? I would still attempt to do something in service of the novel. That would *not* include calling myself dirty names, opting for depression, hitting the bottle, searching out an affair, or abandoning the project (until it really had to be abandoned). I would just try to do some tiny thing in support of the novel, like taking a walk with my notepad in my back pocket, in the hopes that by emptying my mind, my mind would find its way.

I might try to write the scene that I'd been dreading writing. Or I might just sit in front of the blank screen, peel an orange, listen to the too-loud refrigerator, eat the orange slowly, and refuse to budge. Out of frustration, I might take a shower, but with the clear and absolute intention of returning to the same blank screen in fifteen minutes. Or I might write a thousand words, read them over, and discover that I had to discard them. I might write a thousand words, read them over, half-like them and half-hate them, and feel bewildered. Doing such tiny things would hardly guarantee

> *The only thing I know is that if I get to my studio, that means I'm alive today.*
> — ROBERT FARBER

that I'd turn out a masterpiece, but doing nothing would be a sure guarantee that I wouldn't.

What tiny things does an everyday creative person do in support of her creativity? When she has an idea, she writes it down. When she walks down the street and something catches her attention, she is not embarrassed to stop and look. At work, between routine phone calls, she steals a minute, not to play computer solitaire or browse the Internet but to make a quick note in support of the nonfiction book she's writing. When the light at dusk does something to her heart, she pauses to feel it and maybe to capture it. When an opportunity arises at work to do a risky, interesting thing, she takes it. Saying "Yes, I want to do that" is the tiny thing she does, a thing that takes no more than a second or two of her time but that launches a mammoth adventure.

An everyday creative person's whole life is peppered with these tiny events. Out of conscious awareness, her mind is working, and what arrives are those most fleeting of things: thoughts, visions, images, answers. Temporally speaking, each is an infinitesimal thing. It is here, then it is gone. Nor is it a gigantic act to catch that tiny thing; it is much more like the gesture one makes to hook a fish or capture a butterfly. It is the equivalent of a flick of the wrist, yet every invention, every sonata, every intellectual awakening, every romance novel, every Nobel prize–winning answer to a problem in math or physics, starts right there, with that tiny flick of the mental wrist as one captures the fruits of one's own thought processes.

> *To be part of the creation, I must act humbly. I'll take that over a goddess any day!*
> — MAUREEN O'HARA

The thought comes rushing by and you grab it. It all happens in an instant. But so did the Big Bang, another tiny thing of epic proportions.

EXERCISE 8 • *Say "I am a creative person"*

We are at the end of the beginning. I hope that you're already changing into an everyday creative person, someone who feels more comfortable with mystery, who speaks more openly, who uses herself more willingly, who dreams larger, and who works harder at her own pursuits. Here, at the end of the beginning, I'd like you to take a little time to do the following writing. Please fill in these two blanks with at least a paragraph's worth of reflection.

1. "I am a creative person. I would like to set myself the following goals for the coming year . . ."
2. "I am a creative person. In support of these goals, the tiny things I mean to do in the next few days are . . ."

Then, over the next few days, do the tiny things you just described in your last paragraph.

PART 2

Be Human

Weeks 5 - 8

9. Forgive Yourself for All Your Failures

We are born, we grow, and we begin to accumulate successes and failures. We get homework back with a C+ on it or an A-. We are very good at softball, or average, or mediocre. We have the brains for soccer, but not the speed. We make a sketch that our classmate at the next desk laughs at. We are better than average at writing, but still our fourth grade teacher demolishes all of our theme papers.

Our successes are always qualified: we may be fast, but we are not of Olympic caliber; we may have scored well on the SATs, but still only in the high 600s. Our failures, however, feel unqualified, even though they are rarely of any consequence. It doesn't matter at all if our sketch is ugly or if we have no eye for hitting a softball. But for many of us the chance to become an everyday creative person is ground away by these inconsequential failures that subjectively loom so large.

I recently did a consulting session on the phone with a writer in New York. Successful at speechwriting and advertising copywriting, he nevertheless felt that he didn't have it in him to write the novel of his dreams. Like many people, he'd fallen in love with certain writers when he was young, and it seemed to him impossible that he could do what they'd done. Indeed, he'd failed at the two novels he'd written; failed to sell them but, more crucially, failed to write them well.

As I do when I hear such news, I replied, "Congratulations on actually writing those two novels! Now you have your first bad novels behind you! What do you want to write next?" Soon we were laughing. We spent the hour forgiving him for all his supposed sins and planning for his next foray into the unknown.

When we do not forgive ourselves for our past failures—and learn from them, if we can—we end up fearing failure. If we fear failure, we can't create, because our creative efforts will naturally and inevitably bristle with failures. How many rotten sentences will we write? Billions. How many characters will we create who come alive only up to a point? Zillions. How many theories will we propose that cannot be sustained by the facts? Trillions. Our failures could pave a highway to Mars and our successes may barely get us across the room. Should we fear any of that?

I thought my mountain was coming this morning. It was near to speaking when suddenly it shifted, sulked, and returned to smallness. It has eluded me again and sits there, puny and dull. Why?

— EMILY CARR

I can pretty much get the dishes clean every time I do them. I can pretty much pass the time of day by watching a cop drama on TV, even if I've seen it three times before. I can pretty much answer a survey, mail a package, put in my two cents' worth in a discussion about foreign policy. What I can't do is create well every time I go to the computer. No one can. If you take as your model those activities that we all do just fine, like watching television or washing the dishes, then you'll feel like a failure at your creativity. But if you take as your model that rarer way of being— becoming so empty, so curious, so stubborn, and so passionate that calculus or *Hamlet* just comes to you—you'll feel like a success, even though you'll endure a thousand failures. Einstein envisioned relativity but could not create a unified field theory. He was a success and a failure both, like all creators.

EXERCISE **9 A** • *Forgive Yourself for Past*
Mistakes and Failures

Make many little pencil marks on a piece of pa-per, each standing for a past failure. Then erase them one by one. As you do, say, "Maybe that was a failure, but I'm moving on." Erase the violin recital that went sour. Erase the scholarship that you didn't win. Erase the book that you started writing but never finished. Erase the stupid thing you said that cost you a promotion. Erase the ter-rible choice of lover you made. Erase the binge-drinking episode and the six months lost to depression. At the end of the exercise say, "I forgive myself for all of this. I really mean it!"

> *If there were no other proof of the infinite patience of God, a very good one could be found in His toleration of the pictures that are painted of Him.*
>
> — THOMAS MERTON

EXERCISE **9 B** • *Forgive Yourself Right*
Here and Now

Do each of the following things.
Today, make a small drawing. If you like it, fine. If you hate it, forgive yourself. Forgive yourself so completely that nothing remains of your sense of failure.

Tomorrow, write the first paragraph of a short story. If you like it, fine. If you hate it, forgive your-self. Forgive yourself so completely that nothing re-mains of your sense of failure.

The day after tomorrow, dream up a big creative project. If, after thinking about it, you still like it, fine. If you hate it, forgive yourself. Forgive yourself so completely that nothing remains of your sense of failure. Learn to forgive yourself completely, not grudgingly.

10. Forgive Yourself, Period

We began this week by working on forgiving ourselves for all our past mistakes and by pledging to forgive ourselves when we make mistakes in the future. But because most of us are so practiced at self-chastisement and self-denigration, we have a lot more forgiving to work on.

In order to create, we first need to be pardoned. An astonishing number of us have put ourselves on trial, convicted ourselves, and levied the maximum sentence. What were the charges? That we were ordinary. That we didn't have what it took. That other people were less pimply and more graceful. That, as our third grade teacher never let us forget, we were stupid. That we always bumped into things. That we never had a real chance, not with the family fate gave us. That we made the same mistakes not twice but scores and hundreds of times. That we were born inferior and unworthy. Our defense rested early in the trial, and our inner prosecutor really hasn't let up yet.

This conviction takes the form of self-branding. Mary hasn't just procrastinated in the past; she brands herself a procrastinator. Al hasn't just failed to rise to the occasion sometimes; he brands himself a failure. Sue hasn't just acted impulsively now and then; she brands herself out of control. Tom hasn't just backed down a few times; he brands himself a coward. Louise hasn't just not written much yet; she brands herself a no-talent wannabe. This self-branding is done silently, internally, but indelibly, so that when Mary thinks about an interesting project that would require her to work day-in and day-out in a steady way, a voice she cannot hear says, "Procrastinators like you can't manage that, Mary. Forget about it!" When Tom is offered a risky task full of life and a little danger, a voice he cannot hear says, "That's not a job for a coward like you, Tom. Forget about it!" In such ways the past destroys the present and the future.

> *As a child I reacted to stress by developing this compulsion: I would draw an ugly house and then erase the house line by line and turn it into a beautiful one.*
>
> — SYLVIA STONE

But I pardon you.

Do I have the power to free you? Am I governor of the universe, able to commute your sentence? No. I can offer compassion, but only you can do the actual pardoning. Only you can take the time and make the effort to erase those indelible labels, which, thank God, aren't really indelible. What about it? Was yesterday's roast a little on the dry side? Have you let your garden tools rust? Are some of your ideas quite ordinary? Do these and other felonies haunt you? Could there be a better time to forgive yourself? Could there be a better time to sign a blanket pardon?

EXERCISE 10 • *Pardon Yourself*

Creativity is your religion. Your religion is yours to design. You get to make the rules about compassion and forgiveness.

Get a ballpoint pen that clicks. This is your pardon wand. With it you confess your putative sins but also forgive yourself. Whenever you denigrate yourself, get out your pardon wand. Click your pen open. Lay out the charge. "I did nothing of value today." Click your pen shut. Say, "Maybe and maybe not. But in any case, I am forgiven. And I'll do better!" Let the forgiveness ring out. "I am forgiven. And I'll do better!"

Starting tomorrow, use your pardon wand on all the names you call yourself. Maybe you'll get up but not go directly to your creative project, as you hoped you would. Get out your pardon wand. Click it open and say, "I'm undisciplined." Click it shut and say, "Maybe and maybe not. But in any case, I am forgiven. And I'll do better!" See if you can go directly to work then, having forgiven yourself. If you can, you'll have sure proof of the power of self-forgiveness. If you can't, still trust that this exercise is important, and use it every time you call yourself a bad name.

> *It's necessary to constantly remind ourselves that we are not an abomination.*
> — MARLON RIGGS

The day after tomorrow, go a step further. Give yourself a blanket pardon. Yes, you've failed and faltered in many ways. Yes, you might have written several books by now or achieved more with your painting. Yes, there are people to whom you ought to make amends, acts you'd undo if you could, hurdles you'd love a second chance at negotiating. Confessing all that is a brave thing, but the right follow-up is crucial: forgiving yourself and aiming to do better. Click your pen open. "I have been imperfect, even bad." Click your pen shut. "Maybe and maybe not. But I am forgiven. And I'll do better!"

Build forgiveness—and a commitment to do better—into your daily routine.

11. Forgive Others, Too

Blaming ourselves stifles our creativity. But holding a grudge against others has the same stifling effect. If I am consumed with envy, my creativity is consumed in that same conflagration. If all I can think about is that dastardly literary agent to whom I've sent a book proposal and who hasn't responded yet, then that's what I'm thinking about. If I'm dreaming about revenge, I'm not also dreaming about my novel about revenge. If, in short, the pain we experience as we deal with the world takes center stage, then that's the drama we'll be playing and replaying in the theater of our mind.

> *Life being what it is, one dreams of revenge.*
> — PAUL GAUGUIN

There's a profound difference between forgiving others for the sake of our own mental health and letting others harm us. I can forgive a wartime enemy, but perhaps I also have to kill him. Darwin was right when he warned that every animal must watch out for itself, since its survival depends on knowing what wants to eat it for dinner. But the Buddha was right to suggest that a painful thought is less painful if it flashes by than if it attaches to the mind and festers there. A thought that flashes by lasts for no time at all, but a thought that attaches can pester us all day, all week, or even for a lifetime. If I intuit that you're dangerous, I do not come to your house for brunch, but once I've made that decision, I don't think about you at all.

But I'm advocating more than just cleansing the mind of thoughts that serve no useful purpose. I'm also suggesting that when we forgive our putative rivals and enemies, we start to heal ourselves. When you forgive that twelve-year-old painter you see making the television talk show circuit for being wildly successful, even though you've been painting for ten years and no gallery yet represents you, you heal your heart a little and prevent a boulder-size block from getting between you and your work.

I've had it with these cheap sons of bitches who claim they love poetry but never buy a book.

— KENNETH REXROTH

When you forgive your parents for providing your brother with clarinet lessons and jazz camp and not providing you with anything of the sort, you heal your heart a little and can begin studying the clarinet even now. When you forgive others, you heal your own heart.

EXERCISE 11 • *Shorten Your Enemies' List*

Just about everyone maintains an enemies' list. Here is the enemies' list of a hypothetical young short-story writer named Max.

1. The editor at *Redbook,* who rejected my story.
2. The editor at *Harper's,* who rejected my story.
3. The editor at *Playboy,* who rejected my story.
4. The editor at *ZZZ Literary Magazine,* who rejected my story.
5. The literary agent who wrote sarcastically on my query letter before returning it, "Agents don't handle short stories. Grow up!"
6. My day-job supervisor, who wants me to put in extra hours for free.
7. My acquaintance John, whose short story won an O. Henry award.

8. Maureen the short-story writer, who had a book published by Random House.
9. My brother Carl, who works on Wall Street and is rich.
10. My brother's wife, Stacy, who stays at home all day painting and is utterly and blissfully free, while I must go off to my stupid day job.
11. My friend Marlene, who criticized my last story.
12. My mother, who doesn't believe I write that well.

And 99 more. Or is it 99,000?

I hope you see that there's no one on this list who ought to have a place in Max's mind. What would be the point? So I'd suggest to Max that he forgive them all, one by one, with an appropriate forgiveness mantra for each. "Marlene, I forgive you for criticizing my story." "Carl, I forgive you for making so much money." "Ms. literary agent, I forgive you for treating me rudely and highhandedly." "Maureen, I forgive you for having had a book published."

This is your work for the next few days. Write down your own enemies' list. If you can't think of anyone to put on it, that's either terrific news or you're not admitting your own feelings of anger, resentment, and disappointment. In that case, you need to dig deeper. Let the list grow as long as it must. Then, over the next few days, forgive every person on the list, one at a time, not for his or her sake but for your own.

WEEK 6

12. Get Shells in Your Omelette

A lifetime painter knows—but often only after the fact—that the paintings she created while in her twenties were more growth pains than the art she had in her. A lifetime writer knows—but often only after the fact—that his first novel, while poorly plotted and worse written, was still a great success, because he got it finished and could move on to the next thing. A lifetime inventor knows—but only after the fact—that the right metal for his filament was tungsten and not those hundred other metals with which he spent his time and money experimenting.

Mistakes are joyful, truth infernal.
— ALBERT CAMUS

Looking back on so many mistakes, a lifetime creator only smiles. She pats herself on the back and announces, "I got lots of shells in my omelettes. But I never stopped cooking. And look, I did some good work, didn't I?" And she immediately continues, "By the way, I'm going to make more mistakes still! I'm not thrilled to have to confess that, but it's the truth."

One of the hallmarks of an everyday creative person is that she does the kind of work that invites mistakes. She can make a splendid four-cheese omelette, but one day she gets it into her head to include anchovies. Will that taste good? Will that taste awful? Who can say until it's eaten? She can do her job perfectly at work, systematically crossing tasks off her to-do list, but one day she gets it into her head to propose a whole new way of doing things. Is that a good idea? Or a terrible one? Who can say until the new system is up and running?

Not only is she guaranteed mistakes, she guarantees them herself. "You can take it to the bank," she says, "that I'm going to keep making mistakes, because I'm always creating."

EXERCISE **12A** • *Make Some Inedible Omelettes*

L et's make a pair of omelettes.

For the first omelette we'll investigate the idea of "hot." Beat three eggs with a few drops of milk, and get a frying pan hot with a little oil and butter. Put on some gloves and dice twelve habanero peppers, the hottest chili peppers in the world.

The germ of creation even in something that's not good appeals to me.
— JO HANSON

Just in case the idea of "hot" is even hotter than this, let's throw in half a bottle of Tabasco sauce. Stir the peppers into the eggs and drop the mixture into the pan.

When your omelette is ready, remove it to a warm plate. Take a bite about the size of two grains of rice. Have water, bread, and a fire extinguisher handy. Eat. Scream.

This is not a good omelette. This is a mistake of an omelette. You wouldn't serve it in a restaurant. You couldn't sell it. But didn't it do a terrific job of elucidating the idea of "hot"? Isn't it like an all-blue painting, which certainly has a lot to say about blue? Isn't it like a concert without sound, which is odd to pay thirty dollars for but which does a fine job of making an audience desperate for music? Isn't it a really smart, honorable mistake—if it's a mistake at all?

Our second omelette will make us sad. This time, break three eggs into your bowl, shells and all. Prepare your omelette lovingly, even though you know that this is a stupid mistake. Nobody would make this mistake. The world's rankest beginning omelette-maker would know better than to include the shells. But nevertheless here you are, playing the fool. Make the omelette, scorched shells and all, and set it out on a warm plate. Take a good look at it.

You won't want to eat this omelette, but there is a lot to learn from it. This is how we feel after our mistakes. We feel dumb and defeated. But the mistakes aren't the problem. The feelings are. Sigh and dismiss them. Stop picturing egg shells. Go out and have a good meal!

EXERCISE **12B** • *Make a Big Mistake*

Possibly you've been thinking of embarking on some creative project but fear that it would be a bad mistake to try it. Maybe you have the dream of linking up like-minded local sculptors on a single E-mail mailing list, so that the twenty of you could pass news and chat together. But you're stymied because you have the terrible feeling that you'd be making too much work for yourself. Maybe you can envision writing a short story but not something as grand as a novel. Maybe you want to try out an exercise at your next business meeting designed to have people discuss what's on their mind, but fear not knowing how to handle the feelings that might arise. Go ahead anyway and take the risk.

Embark on a project you fear. After three days, evaluate the results. If you've made a tasty omelette, enjoy it. If it's full of shells, rejoice anyway.

WEEK 7

13. Wrestle with Your Demons

Nowhere in this book will you find tips on painting technique or shortcuts to solving tricky calculus problems. The guidance I'm offering has to do with the one who creates—you—and not with the

Your willingness to wrestle with your demons will cause your angels to sing.
— AUGUST WILSON

products of the creative process. Indeed, it's more perplexing now than ever before as to precisely what products you might choose to create. The traditional painting and the traditional sculpture still exist, but so do site-specific installations, earth art, cyber art, multimedia art, even paintings in the snow that are here in the morning and gone by noon.

A creative person can manifest her potential in a bewildering number of ways today, but only if she can manifest that potential at all. My focus is on helping you manifest that potential. If you've been working along, you've now finished six weeks of this program and made some organizational changes and some mental changes, too. This week you'll work on making some additional alterations: getting rid of your demons, those inner voices that distract you, bedevil you, and call you "no good."

To a greater or lesser degree, the following unfortunate process of self-denigration affects each of us. By a very early age we see that we are not perfect. Whether that notion is drummed into us by a critical parent or we just learn it in the course of living, we already know by the time we're ready for preschool that we're human and not godlike. When we have to go to the bathroom, we have to go—no matter how high our IQ. When an angry pit bull approaches we get afraid, no matter how important our friends are or how large our trust fund.

In a million ways we get the message from birth that some perfect being might be in control of all of this, able to hold His bladder for eons and tame fierce dogs with a simple hand gesture, but we aren't in any-thing like such control. For many of us these lessons lead to terrible self-talk. If you're a lucky child, you shrug and say, "Of course. These things are natural. I'm just hu-man." But if you're unlucky and get it into your head that you're to blame for needing a bathroom when your bladder is full or for fearing angry pit bulls—if your natural frailties become internalized as sins—then you end up with an internal chorus of demons ready to undermine your every move.

> *Every new adjustment is a crisis in self-esteem.*
> — ERIC HOFFER

When we are unlucky like this, we don't have to worry about others telling us that we're bound to fail. Betrayed by our own critical self-talk, we've already concluded that we aren't good enough to realize our potential or achieve our dreams.

EXERCISE 13 • *Clean Out Your Refrigerator*

What happens if you don't clean out your refrig-erator? Things go stale and get moldy. Left-overs pile up and every time you shop you increase the clutter. The same is true of your mind. If you don't get rid of your negative self-talk, there's little room left for new thoughts and little chance that you can move forward creatively.

Use the following exercise as a ritual cleansing of your mind, one of the rituals of your new religion. The ritual has three steps.

Step 1. Every morning, as soon as you wake up, say to yourself, "I refuse to bad-mouth myself today."
Step 2. When a particularly powerful or insistent neg-ative thought strikes you, examine it. If it's an objectively true thought, agree with yourself. "It's

hard to write a great novel." "Yes, it is." If, however, the thought is just the equivalent of a slap in the face, vehemently disagree. "I can't write a great novel." "How dare you say that!"

Here are some more examples:

A. Objectively true: "There are many bands out there." *"Yes, there are."*
B. Slap in the face: "My band can't make it." *"How dare you say that!"*
A. Objectively true: "Most new restaurants fail." *"Yes, that's true."*
B. Slap in the face: "My restaurant wouldn't stand a chance." *"How dare you say that!"*

Step 3. Before bed, reflect on the day. Did a demon or two breach your defenses? Quietly say, "Yes, I may have bad-mouthed myself a few times today. But tomorrow I'll do better."

WEEK 7

14. Stop Preening

Ego is a strange word. So is its cousin, narcissism. So is that other family member, pride. These words confuse us because they stand for contradictory ideas. Taking pride in one's work is a good thing but being too prideful to listen to advice is a bad thing. Having that healthy narcissism we call high self-esteem is a good thing, but trampling over others because of our unhealthy narcissism is a bad thing. If by ego we mean a strong sense of self, then ego is something we want. But if by ego we mean a small, defended, preening concern with how we appear, it would be better if we could shed it.

Preening egotism kills creativity. How can you create if the main item on your agenda is to appear "right" at all costs? How can you create if your real goals are to avoid criticism and rejection? How can you create if you're afraid that a good belly laugh will ruin your makeup or that experiencing a deep feeling will threaten your manhood? How can you create if, when you don't get what you want, you find it necessary to note the affront and plot your revenge? Preening kills freedom and wastes precious time.

> *At the museum a troubled woman destroys a sand painting meticulously created over days by Tibetan monks. The monks are not disturbed. The work is a meditation. They simply begin again.*
>
> — SUSAN GRIFFIN

Many people are waiting for their creative products to pour out of them whole. They hope *Wuthering Heights* will magically appear because, if it does, they'll have avoided the ignominy and defeat of miserable first and second drafts. They would rather not write and keep their pride intact than write and wound their pride.

Here are a few of the things I've done out of preening egotism:

- A certain contracted book I was writing needed to be researched, but I didn't want to bother. Wouldn't anything I made up be just as good as the facts?
- A genre novel was going well. All I had to do was obey the rules to end up with a good product. But a third of the way through I said to myself, "Maybe other genre writers have to obey the rules, but not me. I'm sending my characters off on a wild escapade. I'm sure readers will tag along."

- I never attended a writers' conference until I began presenting at them. Ordinary writers attended writers' conferences. Great ones didn't. So what if those writers who attended them were meeting agents and editors, making contacts, and learning the ropes? It was still beneath my dignity to show up.

- I sent out almost illegible copies of a manuscript of a novel (in the days of typewriters and carbon copies) to agents. Since the novel was so good, shouldn't agents exert a little effort to read it? (I can still remember one agent's response: "You're a real writer, but I can barely read this and I can't be bothered.")

There are many wrong kinds of ego, and these are some examples of them. Could you generate a similar list?

EXERCISE 14 • *Egoless Godhood*

Tomorrow you're not going to care how you look. If tomorrow is a work day and you don't dare show up looking like a mess, save this exercise for the weekend.

Dress ratty. Not chic ratty, just ratty. Apply a little dirt to your face. Wipe some mayonnaise from your hand onto your pants. Shake your arms a few times to shake out the notion that you're a pretty important person. Go out, unconcerned about the impression you're making, like a kitten bounding off to play after a long nap.

The day after tomorrow, dress normally but go out with the same attitude: that you're nobody special, just an everyday creative person, someone who creates naturally and un-self-consciously. Bring your notepad, your video camera, or your sketchbook and absolutely no concern about what the world thinks of you.

The day after that, go a step further. Start the day by saying, "I am everything, I am nothing." Spend the day godlike but egoless. In the supermarket, when the checkout line moves too slowly, let go of the mental irritation that, as a special person, you should be served more quickly. On the other hand, when a good idea pops into your head while you're driving home ten minutes later, let go of the mental injunction that you are too ordinary to pull over and write your idea

> *Did not the artists of the great age of Japanese art change names many times during their careers? I like that; they wanted to safeguard their freedom.*
>
> — HENRI MATISSE

down. Refuse to be an unhealthy narcissist, but aspire to be a healthy narcissist. Once you grasp this distinction, you'll be on your way to replacing your defended ego with something infinitely larger and better.

WEEK 8

15. Dispute Boredom

We all get bored from time to time. But usually we prefer not to acknowledge it. To admit to boredom is to invite only one logical response: "So, self, what are you going to do about it?" Of what use would it be to remind yourself that your job is unstimulating, that it wears you out without letting you make use of your talents, and that, if the truth be known, it bores you silly? None, unless you're willing to make a change. How would it improve matters to inform yourself that you're tired of your own stale thoughts and repetitive worries, unless you also had a way to vacuum out your brain and start fresh with a whole new outlook?

When I complained to our preceptor that my frequent mental wanderings were due to boredom, he laughed and told me to think "bored, bored, bored" until the boredom vanished. To my surprise this worked.

— A ZEN STUDENT

If we let ourselves in on the secret that we're bored, we set ourselves up for either depression or for change. Since we're quite aware that change is difficult and full of ramifications, we deny that we're bored, so as to avoid a depression. But denying our truth is ultimately a bad plan, because often the solution to a problem like boredom is just admitting it. If we could just emit one great shout of truthfulness—"I am really bored!"—in the next instant our interest might return. If we could just strike the gong a real blow and let the secret out—"I'm bored! God help me!"—in the next second the sky might regain its awesome look and the desire to create might flood our body. A new thought might enter our head, rather than an old, stale one. Even our job might switch from black and white to technicolor.

As far as boredom goes, we are both victim and culprit. Why the victim? Because we are the fruit of a modern age in which it is hard to maintain meaning. When meaning goes, boredom walks right in. We are also the culprit, because if meaning goes, it is still up to us to retrieve it or to reel in some other meaning. If we don't, we've failed to use our freedom responsibly. Then we're obliged to repeat the words of Dylan Thomas: "Somebody's boring me and I think it's me."

The other day I met with a new client for the first time. She wanted to write a book but her ideas bored her. She described her ideas. I suspect that she wanted me to stop her and exclaim, "Oh, but *that* one sounds interesting!" Maybe she wanted me to agree with her, which of course would have amounted to criticism: "Yes, those *are* pretty boring." Instead I said, "Generate an interesting idea." She shook her head. I smiled and waited. "Can't," she said. "Can," I said. We laughed. Soon she was lost in thought, actu-

> *Every time I think I've touched bottom as far as boredom is concerned, new vistas of ennui open up.*
>
> — MARGARET HALSEY

ally thinking. Then an idea came, as I knew it would, since boredom can't compete with a mind that's turned on and functioning.

EXERCISE **15** • *Your Boredom Meter*

Make a boredom meter out of an oral thermometer. You can also use a forehead thermometer, a plain strip of paper, a candy cane, or anything you like, since all the measurements are intuitive.

Begin by creating a boredom scale: 0 = absence of all interest, utter meaninglessness, living death; 5 = modest interest, occasional creativity, a life neither completely leaden nor really joyous; 10 = passionate interest, flowing creativity, a life bubbling, percolating, cooking. You might want to write out a detailed scale from 0 to 10.

Next, take a baseline boredom reading, one right now and several more over the next few days. Put the boredom meter under your tongue or against your forehead for a minute and then "read" it. How bored do you think you are? Take readings at different times of the day, during different activities, in different rooms of your apartment, at home and at work.

When the number is low, stop everything. Jump up and shout "My God, I'm bored!" Then *do* something. Go immediately to your current creative project and renew its acquaintance. Take your daughter to lunch and renew her acquaintance. Launch a big, new project. Have a small chat with a friend you've been missing. Do something creative or something simply human. Do not sit still and let the numbers on your boredom meter plummet. Remind yourself that not only are you free to do something, but that it's your sacred responsibility. Otherwise you are squandering your freedom.

Take your boredom temperature regularly, especially when you're feeling listless and uncreative. Pick a number that represents all the boredom you'll tolerate in your life—say, seven. Whenever your temperature is eight or higher, celebrate. But when it slips to seven or below, sound your warning bell. Exclaim, "This won't do!" As hard as it might be to move that large object—you—go ahead and make the effort to create and to rejoin the living.

WEEK 8

16. Make an Earth Landing

You may think that we create with our heads, but that's only a part of the story. We create with our feet—by staying put in a certain way—and with our heart—by letting our feelings rise up. You may think that ideas, generated in the head, are the be-all and end-all of a creative effort, but even a master of ideas like Dostoyevsky reaches us the most through his feelings. Did Dostoyevsky write so beautifully about children in *The Brothers Karamazov* because his fine intellect was crackling and sending off sparks? No; it was because the loss of his own child had informed and transformed him. His personal tragedy broke through to his heart, a heart his wife, Anna, had previously doubted could be pierced by anything earthly. What Dostoyevsky learned in sorrow went into his greatest novel.

> *I even think that he is incapable of love; he is too much occupied with other thoughts and ideas to become strongly attached to anyone earthly.*
>
> — ANNA DOSTOYEVSKY

When we can stay put and both feel and think, we can create beautifully. But most of us have terrible trouble sitting still with our own thoughts and feelings. A warning bell goes off: "Better do something, watch a show, read a book, pour some wine, silence is dangerous. In silence, I might start feeling those bad things I've been avoiding." To avoid letting worries, existential doubts, and self-reproaches flood in to fill up the silence, we flutter about, never daring to alight, never daring to grow really quiet.

We are just this unlucky. This inability to sit in silence and think and feel is a function of our modern times. Why do indigenous peoples produce beautiful art? Because they are not anxious in the same way that we are anxious. They can sit in silence and simply connect to their work. A native weaver, sculptor, potter, or musician, who may grow anxious when the owls stop hooting or when a wind comes in from the north, is not sitting in silence wondering "Can I make art? And to what end? And what does it matter anyway, since when I die nothing remains?" He just makes a balanced pot and inscribes the essence of a gazelle. That he can do this reflects no moral superiority or special soulfulness. It's simply that his silence is not bedeviled by all our modern doubts.

A creator's objectives are to stay put, to think,

and to feel. But even the finest artists have real difficulties in this regard. They know how to stay put, but
they are more like moored balloons than rocks. At
any minute their tethers could
loosen and then off they'd fly, like
Dostoyevsky to a gambling episode or Pollock to an alcoholic
binge. Their grounding is perilous
and fragile. Sometimes they can
stay put, think, and feel, but the
next passing cloud, casting a mo-
mentary shadow over existence itself, suddenly uproots them and
sends them packing.

> *Sitting on the floor of a
> room in Japan, looking
> out on a small garden
> with flowers blooming
> and dragonflies hovering
> in space, I suddenly
> felt as if I had been too
> long above my boots.*
>
> — MARK TOBEY

So it is for each of us. An everyday creative person understands that she would love to simply sit still
and make herself available for thoughts and feelings,
her thoughts soaring and her feelings bringing her
back to earth, so that her creative work becomes
grounded in the human condition and rooted in reality. But the workings of her own anxious modern
mind threaten and endanger her.

EXERCISE 16 • *Have Lunch in a
Hospital Cafeteria*

There is no better place to stay put, think, and feel
than among people who are going about their
everyday business. This is why writers seek out cafes;
this is why, for the next three days in a row, you'll
have lunch in a hospital cafeteria. (If you can't make
it to a hospital cafeteria, try a bus station, a hotel
lobby, or a busy library—any place that is a hive of
human activity.)

The hospital cafeteria meals won't cost you much
and you'll be surrounded by reality, by people hurt-

ing, by people healing, by tired caregivers and families bearing flowers. Pick a table right in the middle of things, right next to that irritable cougher, the one who's agitated because he can't smoke inside. As you sit there, think of real things: your real mother, your real father, real deaths, real miscarriages. Feel the weight of the world resting on your shoulders and on all those shoulders around you.

As you sit, the silence punctuated by loudspeaker calls for doctors, imagine a project that illuminates some aspect of the human condition. Maybe it's a poem; maybe it's volunteer work; maybe it's an essay; maybe it's a letter to your father. Commit to the project for these three days, thinking about it and even working on it some. At the end of the three days decide whether or not to continue pursuing it. My hunch is that you'll be tempted, since, if you've spent these three lunch hours grounded and open, what arose is probably a rich and worthwhile project.

PART 3

Be Mindful

Weeks 9 - 12

17. Rouse Out of Your Dream Sleep

Many religions, Buddhism and the religion of creativity among them, concern themselves with mindfulness. By mindfulness I mean the art of pure attention and the skills of critical thinking. Let's examine the concept of mindfulness by considering the possibility that we spend too much of our life in a kind of dream sleep, going through the motions, and too little of it in a state of genuine wakefulness. If we're honest with ourselves, I think we'd all agree that we feel really alert and awake only a small portion of the time.

By chance I fell into the dust net of this world where in an instant passed some thirty years.

— T'AO CH'IEN

When I was twenty-two and a student at the University of Oregon, I bought some foreign coins at a fair. I don't know why, since I had next to no money and actually hated the idea of collecting things. It bothered me that I had bought them, and a year later, when I was living in Boston, I decided to sell them. I went to a coin store. The owner was busy and, while I waited, a man sidled up to me. He asked me if I had coins to sell. I said that I had. I showed them to him and he made me quite a reasonable offer.

The only problem was, he had no money. He wondered if I would take a ride with him to his bank. Only an idiot would have. I did. In the car he regaled me with stories. He was by profession a monkey collector who spent most of his time in South America snaring monkeys for medical labs, which was why he was in the Boston area, delivering his monkey supply. We went to his bank; odd to say, it had just closed. So he proposed the following plan. He would take the coins and I would take his watch, which he put a very nice dollar value on, and we would meet outside the coin shop the following day to complete the transaction. Only an idiot would have agreed to this plan. I did.

> *A man that is born falls into a dream like a man who falls into the sea.*
>
> — JOSEPH CONRAD

That next afternoon, standing in front of the coin shop, waiting for the monkey hunter who I knew wasn't coming, I awoke from youth. I could feel my eyes open as I stood there. The longer I waited, the more fully I roused from my dream sleep. It seems to me now that I accompanied that monkey hunter for exactly that reason, to be taken in and awakened, because somehow intuitively I knew that I was in a young man's deep sleep that had to end if I was going to grow and live. The next day I started writing my first novel.

How can we wake ourselves from our dream sleep? Sometimes trauma or drama causes that awakening, as when a heart attack strikes a loved one, a fire burns down our house, a war breaks out, or we're diagnosed with a fatal illness. All of a sudden our eyes open and we see that we've been running in an endless race that we never consciously entered. Now that our eyes have opened, we want to stop running. We want to do new things. We want to do things differently, consciously, more deeply, less automatically.

What else wakes us up? Sometimes a chance encounter with a monkey hunter. But our best bet is to maintain a real and constant vigilance, by regularly pricking ourselves with a pin, metaphorically speaking, and inquiring of ourselves, "Am I asleep or am I awake?" If the answer is "asleep," try the following exercise.

EXERCISE **17** • *Shout "Wake Up!"*

What happens if you try to rouse people from their dream sleep? Usually they keep on sleeping. Maybe you give them a harder nudge. If they're like me, not a darned thing happens. They won't roll over, they won't stir at all. Nudges won't rouse people caught in a deep life sleep.

Today go to the mirror and start shouting at yourself. "Wake up! Wake up, damn it!" Shout loud enough that your neighbors call the police. When the police come, explain yourself: "I've been in a deep sleep, which has kept me from my creative work. I'm screaming to wake myself up." If they think you're loony, show them this book.

"Dear officer: this person is following my orders by shouting. I am a licensed therapist. Thank you."

There. That should do it.

Tomorrow, ask yourself the question: "Am I asleep?" See how you answer it. If the answer is no, celebrate. If the answer is yes, spend a few minutes discussing with yourself what would wake you up and what you would do if you were awake.

The day after tomorrow, be awake all day. See if you understand what that means. See how that feels. See if you can do it.

WEEK 9

18. Lose Your Self-consciousness

The mind, despite its largeness, can be reduced to little more than a barely functioning machine if we aren't careful. Imagine a mighty landscape crisscrossed by narrow gullies. Some majestic animals get to stroll about the whole landscape, while other small, hardy, but frightened animals run up and down those dry gullies, hiding from view and endlessly retracing their steps. When I think expansively and am not worrying about me, I get to live in that landscape. But when I can only think about me, about how I am suffering or what I am missing in life, I consign myself to a dry gully. In the first instance, I am conscious; in the second, I am self-conscious.

> *All great work—artistic, poetic, intellectual or spiritual—is produced at those moments when creators forget themselves altogether and are free from self-consciousness.*
> — WALPOLA RAHULA

Self-consciousness is an inordinate concern about the self, arising from fears and worries. When we feel unsafe, we obsess about safety and can't think expansively. When we feel we have nothing to offer but our looks, we obsess about our looks and not the look of the landscape around us. When we feel too anxious about speaking in public, we obsess about our upcoming public speaking engagement; we don't have mind space left to produce a mighty speech. When we feel incompetent, we obsess about making mistakes, being found out, and failing. No neurons are left for dreaming big.

In all these cases, the focus of attention is on the self, which feels threatened and needy and can only concentrate on itself. At the extreme, this big thing—the mind—is reduced to thinking about one thing over and over again. If it's paranoia that the mind hooks itself onto, it repeats itself as follows: "Who is out to get me? Is it my boss? He looked at me oddly. Is it my old boyfriend, who I think used to love me but I now think hates me? Who is out to get me? And why? What have I done? Why are they all threatening me? Why have they been threatening me all my life? What have I done? Why are they out to get me?"

Most of us allow our thoughts to hook themselves onto certain thematic fears and worries too much of the time. We're concerned about something—something at work, something with our mate, something we dread, something we didn't get—and end up minding ourselves and our worries to the exclusion of everything else. Like a bout of illness, this dreaded self-absorption, rooted in worry, can strike at any time. Human beings are as susceptible to self-consciousness as they are to colds.

Inspiration may be a form of super-consciousness or perhaps of subconsciousness: I wouldn't know. But I am sure it is the antithesis of self-consciousness.

— AARON COPLAND

My wife and I have some friends, a married couple, Jill and Michael. Jill had an uncle, an elderly man of modest means with no other living relation but his niece Jill. Frail and unwell, he married a very rich woman, herself frail and unwell. If the uncle died first, his wife, when she died, would leave her money to charity. But if she died first, the uncle would get the money, and then, in due course, it would go to Jill and Michael. This was terrible luck for our friends, who could think about nothing else than "We might be rich soon. We might be rich soon. We might be rich soon." Of course they also thought, "Please let her die first," and "Hold on, Uncle," and "This is crazy, obsessing about wealth when we never even cared about money."

When you obsessively think about you, that is self-consciousness. Self-consciousness kills creativity. Each of us needs to find a cure for the doubts, fears, worries, feelings of resentment, and other viruses that produce this unhealthy and unproductive state of mind.

EXERCISE 18 • *Healing a Troubled Mind*

Some time today you will notice that you're worry-ing about something. When that worry arrives, imagine that you can pluck it from your head and move it wherever you want. Have a Ziploc bag handy. Open it, drop that worried thought in, zip the bag back up, and return it to your pocket. Then say, "I'm quite well."

This is brain surgery.

When you have your next worried thought, do ten jumping jacks. Then say, "I'm quite well."

This is physical therapy.

When your third worried thought arrives, visu-alize it shrinking, as a healing tumor would shrink. Then say, "I'm quite well."

This is attitudinal healing.

For the next three days, every time a worried thought arrives try out a new cure.

WEEK 10

19. Use Your Brain

When a teacher asks her student a question, she wants an answer, not a debate about the mer-its of her question. Parents seek obedience from their children, not arguments about the virtues of clean rooms versus messy rooms or the legitimacy of their traditional religion versus other religions. Employers ask their employees to watch the bottom line, not to wax philosophical about capitalism.

Not much in the experience of growing up or living in the world helps hone a person's critical thinking skills. If I asked you to evaluate the effectiveness of one parenting style versus another, to argue the merits of the two sides in the pro-life/pro-choice debate, or to decide which group of experts in a controversy ought to be believed, would you know where to begin? Probably not. Most of us are not trained to think critically, and, as a rule, not even permitted to think critically, either by our culture or by the demands of our personality. The culture says, "Quick, what's your opinion?" Our brain says, "Look, it's too troubling and confusing to think about matters deeply. Let's just make a choice, arrive at a conclusion, and get on with things."

Knowing is false understanding. Not knowing is blind ignorance.
— NAN CH'UAN

We should have been taught critical thinking skills throughout our school years and surely somewhere in our college curriculum. But during my undergraduate degree program in philosophy, for instance, such teaching was nowhere to be found. We spent whole semesters on medieval ontological arguments and on linguistic analysis, but not one day on bedrock questions like "What's a fact and what's an opinion?"; "How do we weigh evidence?"; or "By what means do we select among choices?"

I now teach critical thinking skills to adults who frequently realize after one evening of instruction that they have never learned this material before. They have never spent time really comparing and contrasting viewpoints. They have never tried to articulate their reasons for choosing one thing over another. They have never realized that, in order to evaluate something, you first need to identify and rank your criteria of evaluation. On the one hand, they're upset to discover that their education failed them and that they might have done much better work in school if they had been taught how to think. On the other hand, they're excited by learning new skills and watching their own thinking improve on the spot.

> *His mind is furnished as hotels are, with everything for occasional and transient use.*
>
> — GEORGE ELIOT

A complete definition of "creativity" would include an awful lot, among which would certainly be the ability to think critically. To write your novel as it ought to be written, you have to read it and revise it with a critical eye. To judge whether your theory is making sense, you have to apply critical thinking skills. To know whether your painting is finished or still needs work, you have to evaluate it. Every so often a very creative person, interviewed because he or she is so creative, will reply to the question "What is creativity?" with some variation of the following: "It's just using your brain." This can't be the whole definition of creativity but, as short answers go, it's still the best one. Improving our critical thinking skills is the surest way to unleash our creativity.

EXERCISE 19 • *Analyze Events*

Once a day for the next three days, analyze an event.

Say that you're walking along and see someone go out of his way to pick up a discarded Pepsi can. Stop and jot down as many of the things that action might signify as you can dream up. Here's what my partial list might look like:

1. The person who's picked up the can is anal and compulsive.

2. He's bored and lonely.
3. He's community-minded.
4. He's poor and needs the money he'd get from re-cycling the can.
5. He's building a Pepsi-can sculpture.
6. He's on a mission from God.
7. He's on a psychotic mission from an invented God.
8. He plans to use the Pepsi can for adornment.
9. He's running for office.
10. He's addicted to Pepsi and hopes a few drops are left in the can.
11. He works for Coke and is determined to rid the world of all traces of Pepsi.

Spontaneous analyzing is its own creative act. You get to use your imagination, your intuition, your critical thinking skills, your brain in all its glory. Over the next three days, go in for spontaneous analysis.

WEEK 10

20. Understand a Frog Thoroughly

If there's anything we should be able to understand thoroughly, it's ourselves. We live with ourselves for every minute we are alive, we watch ourselves and see how we operate, our brains have an excellent self-reflective apparatus built right in, we possess nuanced words with which to describe ourselves and paper and pencils with which to write down what we've learned. We should be able to assess our capabilities, recognize our flaws, understand our desires and motives, and basically know ourselves inside and out.

But we don't. We still marry people we have to divorce a week later and work in jobs that hold no meaning for us. For all our gifts, we do pretty poorly at self-awareness. A client will tell me, "I'm not paint-ing a lot, but it doesn't worry me. That's my process. I'm a slow in-cubator." A year later he'll finally admit, "I'm not painting a lot, and that's a problem." Another client will say, "I had a chance to sing at an open-mike night but I

> *When you understand a frog through and through, you attain enlightenment.*
>
> — SHUNRYU SUZUKI

didn't take it. Maybe it was too hot inside the club." By the end of the session she's willing to admit, "I guess singing in public scares me." Sometimes it seems as though we lie so much to ourselves that we need to train as spies in order to obtain self-information.

It would be wonderful if we were more self-transparent. We're like the quintessential tragic hero, born great, full of astounding qualities, but opposed to self-scrutiny. When warning bells go off—don't murder Duncan, don't compound that sin by killing Banquo—we hear those bells in a muffled way; worse, we aren't interested in what they signify. If we were truly interested, we'd stop everything and ex-claim, "I need to listen closely." But instead we don't paint and we refuse to consider why, we don't sing and we blame our reluctance on a broken air condi-tioner. The better plan, and one each of us is capable of putting into action, is to find the courage to look into the mirror and understand ourselves thoroughly.

EXERCISE 20 • *Examine Some Accusations*

Think of ten people who know you. Ask yourself the following question: "What would each of them say about me?"

Probably you don't want to do this.

Let's stop for a second and analyze what's troubling you. If you hadn't a clue what other people would say about you, if you had to scratch your head and really think about the matter, the exercise wouldn't bother you. But the truth is that you already know that many of them would have one or another charge to level against you. Marvin would call you lazy. Sally would call you neurotic. Larry, who's a prolific writer, would sneer at your paltry literary output. Your mother would shake her head and wonder how you managed to gain all that extra weight. Your teachers from grammar school would say things like "very ordinary" and "I don't remember her." One by one, they'd break your heart.

> For the ordinary man, whose mind is a checkerboard of criss-crossing reflections, opinions, and prejudices, bare attention is virtually impossible.
>
> — PHILIP KAPLEAU

It's that broken heart we fear.

But once we realize that, we can deal with the fear better. We have less need to plug up our ears to keep out our mom's criticism or Larry's sarcasm. We can even do a better job of looking at ourselves in the mirror. So go ahead: write down what you think each of ten people who know you would say about you.

Some of their comments may be positive and some negative. Pick three of the negative ones and spend a little time dealing with them.

Today, take the first accusation—say, that you're lazy. Invent a few characters and draw a cartoon strip about laziness, examining the theme and learning something about the problem.

Tomorrow, take the second accusation—say, that you're fat—and write a short scene for a one-act play about it. Is the central character's obesity an obsession, a passion, a ploy, a habit, a matter of indifference? Think about it.

The day after tomorrow, take the third accusation—say, that you're ordinary—and write a song about it, the lyrics and the music both. Don't try to deny the charge or defend yourself. Just think about "ordinariness," investigate it in a song, and go around singing it.

One of the goals of an everyday creative person is to understand herself thoroughly. If she's able to accomplish that goal she'll spot some quite-unwelcome sights in her own being, sights that now and then will drive her to despair. But by the same token she'll also live more freely, truthfully, and creatively.

WEEK 11

21. Study One Blade of Grass

We ended last week with some intense study of the self. Let's begin this week with another aspect of mindfulness: intense study of the natural world.

What might venturing out into nature and studying a blade of grass, a poppy flower, or a bamboo stalk have to do with creativity? If you're a visual artist and your subject matter is nature, the connections are easy to see. But what if you're starting a consulting business, designing websites, or studying higher mathematics? Why should you bother meditating on a weed or examining how a tree branch bends?

The main reason is a very deep one. We've been built to live in this world, to eat pumpkin pie and need the sun, to enjoy a swim in a lake and to go for long walks. We are, as the neurophilosophers say, not just brains, but fully embodied creatures. Sitting in our office cubicle or our studio we tend to forget this. It is much harder to be mindful of the world of which we are a part when we remain only a mind, floating in cyberspace from spreadsheet to chat room, divorced from the elements. It isn't that we aren't built to live in high rises and to breathe their artificial air, too, since we've clearly adapted to both. But occasionally we need to step outside and let an apple fall on our head.

> *If we look at a Japanese artist, we see a man who is undoubtedly wise. What does he spend his time doing? Studying a single blade of grass.*
>
> — VINCENT VAN GOGH

There is no doubt that we can think indoors, and if creativity were just about thinking we could live in a pickle jar on life support and keep on producing ideas. But what sort of ideas would we produce if we never saw a gull dive into the sea, never saw a bleached bone in the desert sand, never saw the silhouette of an oak against the skyline at dusk? We are embodied creatures and we come from the natural world, and it's no wonder that Mozart's music so often came to him during carriage rides in the woods.

There's a second profound reason to study a blade of grass. Too often, we leap to the totality of a thing without giving any mind to its constituent parts. We declare that we are for or against a war without knowing who we are bombing or what the bombing is intended to do. We make pronouncements about the nature of life without observing how other life forms—earthworms, bats, viruses—spend their days and nights. When we set out to study a single blade of grass (or a single protein molecule, a single asteroid, a single customer reaction, a single character we've dreamed up) we are reminding ourselves that great edifices are built out of actual building blocks.

EXERCISE **21** • *Study a Single Blade of Grass*

Today, study a blade of grass for several minutes. Go out, find some tall grass, sit down, select a blade, and give it your undivided attention. If you can't get out, study a leaf or stalk of the potted plant in your living room or office cubicle.

What should you be thinking about or noticing? If you can actually quiet your nerves and your chattering mind and pay attention to the blade of grass to the exclusion of everything else, you will know without having to ask what this exercise is designed to do.

Tomorrow, focus on your own creative work. If you're a musician, focus on one note for several minutes. Play a scale and from that scale select a note that moves you. Then keep playing it. Play it long and short, soft and loud, lilting and staccato. Study that one note for a good long time. Then, if you feel like it, study another note, maybe one you feel complements the first one.

If you're an actor, focus on one feeling or quality, say "jealousy" or "indifference." Whenever you have the chance during the day, react jealously or indifferently to the everyday situations that arise. Try out some nuanced differences. React with insane jealousy at the sight of your coworker's beautiful new shade of lip gloss but with only the barest hint of jealousy to her hefty pay raise.

If you're a writer, select a word with a lot of resonance for you—it might be "spirit," "teacher," "pain," "love," "money"—and focus on it by writing it in huge letters on one of your erasable boards.

Stand in front of it for fifteen minutes and just think about it. Go away, come back again a few hours later, and think about your word some more.

The day after tomorrow, write a little on the theme, "a single blade of grass." Write about parts and wholes, brilliant bits and great master works, solitary ideas and the theories into which they are spun. As you write, recollect that single blade of grass.

> *While drawing grasses I learn nothing "about" grass, but wake up to the wonder that there is grass at all.*
> — FREDERICK FRANCK

WEEK 11

22. Analyze

Very often a new client will say to me, "I have so many creative projects in mind that I don't know where to begin. So I haven't begun." My invariable response is, "Well, let's examine those projects." This response surprises clients, who probably are thinking "He's going to say I'm just making excuses" or "I suppose he'll want to hear about my childhood." They may indeed be making excuses, and their inability to choose among their potential projects may indeed connect to their upbringing. But the simpler possibility is that they find careful examination—or analysis—scary and difficult and therefore prefer not to do it.

Instead of analyzing where the plot for our screenplay should go, we repeat the plot of *Star Wars*. Instead of analyzing the literary marketplace, we proclaim that we're creating for our own enjoyment and don't need to know who buys what. Instead of laying our projects out in front of us and deciding which is the best one to tackle, we throw up our hands and exclaim, "I just have too many ideas! I am too fertile!"

Medical doctors were the subject of an interesting psychological experiment. A group of doctors was supplied with data about two hypothetical hospitals and told that, for financial reasons, only one hospital could remain open. Which one should it be? Each doctor in the group weighed the data and came to a decision. A second group of doctors was supplied with data about three hypothetical hospitals and again told that only one could remain open. Faced with much more data and three possible choices, these doctors had profound difficulty in choosing. Most let all three hospitals stay open, even though that wasn't an option. In essence, they threw up their hands. "There's too much to analyze here! Leave me alone!"

> *There's a tension in deciding what to choose from the real landscape and what to say about it.*
> — MARION BRYANT

Just the other day, a new client complained that he had six books he wanted to write. I surprised him by asking him to tell me about each one. One was about the mentoring relationship between an old Jewish man and a young Jewish boy. He described it to me, and I wondered aloud if a quiet first novel with little plot and no particular appeal for women could be sold today. If the author were Roth, Mailer, or Heller . . . but the client wasn't. His second novel was the story of an unsympathetic ad executive, set against a backdrop of advertising industry unscrupulousness. Here, again, I had my doubts. Could an unknown writer interest editors in a topic that might not interest many readers, that had a main character with whom it was hard to identify, and that had an unhappy ending to boot? Maybe, but the long odds certainly had to be factored into the equation.

The fifth novel turned out to be much more exciting. Even so, we concluded that the hero's character had to be altered in order for the novel to work. Then suddenly the book rose head and shoulders above the others. A few days later I received a letter. "I leaped out of bed at six this morning, grabbed a legal pad, and began scribbling," my client wrote. "Just before I woke up I had an image that told me where to begin. That's never happened to me before. I spent the next hour brainstorming and came away elated. Now I have a strong sense of where the novel might take me."

> *One reason my paintings have become realistic has to do with my interest in what things really look like.*
> — ROBERT BECHTLE

Analysis opened the sluice gate. Then creativity flooded in.

EXERCISE **22** • *Analyze*

Today, imagine you're writing an adventure novel. Your hero will find himself in many tight scrapes. Dream up seven of those scrapes and pick items from your desk to get him out of them. The phone receiver could be a bludgeon, the Mickey Mouse pen an eye gouge, the Frappuccino bottle a vehicle for a message. Analyze the items on your desk for their lethal appeal and, if the exercise incites you, start writing your adventure novel.

Tomorrow, analyze a painting, a movie, or a procedure at work. For instance, look up Renoir's *Luncheon of the Boating Party* in an art book. Critics consider it a masterpiece. Can you tell why its formal composition is so harmonious? (Hint: it has to do with the way an ellipse can be drawn through the heads of the party goers.) Or you could analyze a piece of music, your manager's supervisorial style, your building's architecture, or your sister's parenting style. Select something and make a sincere effort to understand it.

The day after tomorrow, think about your current creative project. What about it ought to be analyzed? Where would an application of your critical thinking skills prove useful?

WEEK 12

23. Synthesize

Imagine that you're sitting outside in a park, maybe nodding off a little, when suddenly a strange animal bounds by. A moment later, a bearded fellow drives up in a van, gets out, approaches you, and issues the following command. "You are to build the animal you just saw. Here in the back of the van are the parts you'll need. Maybe all the parts are there, maybe they're not. Actually, it may turn out that none of the parts is right. On the other hand, everything you need may be there. Go ahead and begin."

You look inside the van and see nothing that looks particularly useful. Instead of a collection of eyes, hooves, and tails, out of which you might take a shot at recreating the animal you saw, you see swatches of fabric, shiny washers, computer motherboards, rolls of iron mesh, neat piles of zinc, magnesium, and selenium, and cans with labels like "liver molecules" and "muscle memory." What would you do? Let's say that your life depended on it. Could you make sense of such an absurd and motley collection of things?

Some percentage of the time this is exactly what goes on when we attempt to create. Inside our brain, synthetic operations occurring out of conscious awareness culminate in synthetic moments, and all of a sudden we see a strange animal bound by, hear a symphony, or realize that the sun can't possibly be revolving around the earth. If we're not too frightened by our revelation, we embark upon a second series of synthetic operations, sometimes called the "elaboration phase" of the creative process, during which we try to prove our hypothesis, build our beautiful animal, or write our symphony.

> *Life sucks order from a sea of disorder.*
> — JAMES GLEICK

However, we don't and can't know if our original vision was accurate, or accurate but not worth pursuing (who needs this new animal anyway, when there are so many stray cats and dogs needing adoption?), or whether it was accurate and worthy but unrealizable with the materials available in our neural supply store. So we set out to synthesize but we embark doubtfully and reluctantly, because we intuit just how many land mines are laid out between our vision and its realization.

Another significant percentage of the time we have even less of a starting point. No animal bounds by. All we have is our desire to create. We wake up and say, "This is a creating day," but nothing is percolating inside of us. How do we synthesize when we have no vision for reference? How do we write a book when we have no book idea? How do we start an E-business when we have no E-business idea? How do we begin a painting when all we have are tubes of pigment lined up in front of us? If you say to yourself, "Without an idea or a model for reference I can't begin, so I'd better wait for an animal to bound by," you've thrown the day away. So there must be a better plan.

In Zen brush-painting, the circle is a master's problem. It represents everything and nothing, and in so doing, the universe.

— MICHAEL TODD

The better plan—whether or not you have a starting point—is to trust your natural synthesizing abilities. If you sit quietly and say, "Come, E-business," a billion neurons will begin scurrying about, pressed into service. From the left will come a vision of a whitewashed villa on the Riviera. From the right will come a picture of a beautiful San Francisco loft space. They'll collide and you'll get the message: "home exchange." Your E-business will have begun.

EXERCISE 23 • *Practice Synthesizing*

For the next few days, practice synthesizing. Today, cut a hundred random words out of a magazine. Take some from the advertisement pages, some from the feature articles, some from the editorial columns. Lay the words out on the rug and create a paragraph. Discard the words that don't seem to fit and cut out any new ones you need.

Tomorrow, list twenty random ideas (like photosynthesis, trickle-down economics, the hero's journey, urban planning, nature/nurture, abstract expressionism, etc.) and use your odd array to create a fine theory. Again, you can discard the ideas that don't fit and add any new ones you need.

The day after tomorrow ask yourself, "What does my creative life need?" Grow quiet and let your brain make some deep connections. See what arises. It might be, "You need to work harder." It might be, "You need to make a plan and keep to it." It might be an image, a word, a jingle, an injunction. If the message that arrives feels useful, use it.

24. Lose Yourself

In the religion of creativity, as in Zen, we have lovely paradoxical-sounding maxims. An important one is "lose yourself in order to find yourself."

Picture the following. A party is going on. Many lively, interesting conversations are taking place, along with a few deadly dull ones. In one corner sits a visitor from a foreign land who is patiently waiting to be acknowledged and invited to speak. She is a genius who can play beautiful piano sonatas, amaze listeners with her spoken words, or let them in on a cure for cancer if they're interested, but first she needs silence in the room. Since she won't assert herself and ask for silence, and since that silence will never come of its own accord, she patiently sits in the corner, awaiting her opportunity, for all eternity.

What's needed? A host: someone aware of the value of this guest, able to quiet the others, and willing to intercede on everyone's behalf. Someone is needed who will say, "Excuse me, can I have a little quiet! Can we lose the chatter?" Someone is needed who, once silence is obtained, will inquire of our foreign visitor, "Do you need anything? A piano? A microphone? A glass of water?" and who then steps aside and turns the podium over to our visitor.

This guest from afar, our inner genius, needs silence if she is to operate. Inner noise—worries, doubts, rages, fears, and other distracting thoughts and feel-ings—can prevent our inner ge-nius from functioning. Losing yourself means taking it upon yourself to quiet those noisy in-ternal guests so that the little ge-nius in the corner can take center stage. You lose the noise in order to gain your own genius.

> *To be happy in the world, it is necessary to feel oneself part of the stream of life flowing from the first germ to the remote and un-known future.*
>
> — BERTRAND RUSSELL

A client named Jim once complained about his band. The drummer was too old, the bassist wore his hair funny, the lead guitarist had switched from grass to heroin, and club owners always stiffed them when it came time to pay. Things of that sort, which never escaped Jim's attention, were, in his estimation, killing the band's chances for success. But I wondered aloud if Jim's band's lack of success didn't have more to do with the fact that, as he himself explained it, they had no original songs to play and the songs they did play they played without passion. Which was more im-portant, the drummer's age and the bassist's hairdo or the band's lack of energy, pur-pose, skill, and originality?

Jim needed to write good songs and not concern himself with his drummer's age. He needed to find an enthusiastic bassist, not worry about changing his current bassist's hair style. He needed to refocus his attention,

> *It's unnecessary and destructive to think of oneself at all. People ask me, "What do you think of yourself as?" My answer is, "Nothing."*
>
> — PAUL BOWLES

which for safety's sake was obsessing about minutia, and instead face the bigger questions, the ones that produce keener anxiety, and gain his own creativity in the process. He needed to lose his current brain, with its defensiveness, in order to gain his better brain, his whole brain, the one that knew how to write songs, choose band members, and electrify an audience.

EXERCISE 24 • *Throw Out Some Mental Trash*

Imagine a big Dumpster like the ones you see in front of houses undergoing major renovations. Then take a look at the following list. On it are some (but not all) of the kinds of mental trash that it is in our best interest to lose. Choose three items you'd like to eliminate from your own mind.

- fear
- anger
- anxiety
- doubt
- guilt
- irritability
- ego
- memories of failure
- envy
- lack of confidence

Today, imagine taking the first item down to the Dumpster. Picture yourself filling up a large garbage bag with all the guilt or irritability that's currently burdening you, carrying it down to the Dumpster, and tossing it away. Tomorrow, rid yourself of the second item. The day after, get rid of the third. If you have more trash to eliminate, visualize throwing it away, too. When you've taken all the bags down, picture the Dumpster being removed by a big truck and with it all of your mental trash.

PART 4

Explore

Weeks 13-16

25. Explore

Huckleberry Finn escapes his father's clutches and heads down the Mississippi River in order to save himself. He rebels against the rules of his culture—that he go to school, that he attend church, that he obey his father—and, by lighting out, opts for adventure and exploration instead. *Huckleberry Finn* is a great yarn, but it is also a metaphor for the creative journey, which requires that we escape the clutches of everyday thinking and culturally determined behaving and explore life in a personal way, seeking out adventures of the mind and actual adventures. We need to explore bayous so as to paint them and to experience sunsets so as to write about them.

> *I don't go into the studio with the idea of "saying" something. What I do is face the blank canvas and put a few arbitrary marks on it that start me on some sort of dialogue.*
>
> — RICHARD DIEBENKORN

Our subject for this month is exploration. Few of us do enough exploring. When we were very young, a day came when we took our crayons and used them on every surface we could find. I know that I used them on the pages of my brother's stamp collection, because those pages still exist and every so often I happen upon them. We unbridled toddlers would take our crayons and try them out on the bathroom mirror, the wallpaper, the parquet floor, the plastic slipcover entombing the living room sofa, even on white bread and other really unsuitable surfaces.

We explored and learned an awful lot that way and were on our way to a lifetime of creating, the heart of which is trial-and-error exploration. But our parents got wind of what we were up to and halted our efforts. Children who were punished for writing on walls and had their crayons taken away—rather than being graced with a wry smile and given reams of paper for their further explorations—had their ability to explore and their desire to create undermined. For many people, those early years at home and at school did little to encourage their instinct for exploration.

Now we need to explore again, if we are to create. A good place to start is with the love that prompted us those many years ago to see how red crayon marks looked on cream-colored wallpaper: that is, with our love of color.

EXERCISE **25** • *Explore Color*

Stop by an art supply store and buy three tubes of acrylic paint: one cobalt blue, one aquamarine, and one white. Also buy some cheap student canvas boards, shrink-wrapped in packages of three, or a sketch pad, some palette paper, and a cheap brush or two. All of this shouldn't cost you too much money.

Today, you're going to make some blues. You're not out to paint irises or blue mountains, you're just exploring blue, doing a little color homework. Squeeze out some of the cobalt or aquamarine paint onto your palette paper. Look at it. Squeeze out a little white. Is it white like whitewashed walls or white like soft-serve ice cream? Mix a little of the blue with a little of the white. You've made a new color. Look at it. Make a mark with it on your canvas or sketch paper. Make blue marks until there is no more blue left on the bristles of your brush. Then clean your brush.

Mix a second blue, using a little more or a little

less white, or combining the aquamarine and the cobalt. Mark with it. Notice the mark your full brush makes and the one it creates when it's half empty. Does the blue seem different when you paint up and down and when you paint side to side? What happens when the new blue touches the old one? Do you get three blues, one blue, or many? Encircle some blue with white. Encircle some white with blue. Make a hundred shades, a hundred hues, and a host of marks, some like blue animal tracks, some like blue ivy growing.

Look at life with the eyes of a child.
— HENRI MATISSE

Spend a little time naming the blues you've created. Blues already have names like bronze blue, Berlin blue, Antwerp blue, celestial blue, Chinese blue, steel blue, Milori blue. Name yours. Name the one in the middle of the canvas for the lake you used to visit with your parents. Name the one off to the left for dusky skies in winter. Name the one you made blue lines with for the blue veins just above your wrist.

Tomorrow, explore your current creative project. If you're composing Latin fusion tunes, spend an hour sampling your tango collection. If you're blocked on your dissertation, explore your hypothesis. If you've been feeling unmotivated to complete your statue, explore some interesting anatomical structure: say spines, from the spinelike filaments in deep-sea creatures, to the outrageous spines of dinosaurs, to your own spine. Make "explore" one of the sacred words of your religion.

26. Ask One Question

You can jump start your creativity in the following way:

1. Ask yourself an interesting question.
2. Try to answer it.

As simple as this is to say, it is anything but easy to arrive at deep questions worth our devotions or to answer them adequately once we get them framed. Many complications arise. We may unwittingly impose an answer on the question because of some agenda we have, rather than engaging in honest inquiry. For example, our desire to prove or disprove the existence of the unconscious will surely color the way we answer our own provocative question, "What is meant by the unconscious?" We may ask a question that has no answer, or that has several competing answers, or that was framed just incorrectly enough that we can't get started answering it. These are the kinds of difficulties that confront everyday creative people who take it upon themselves to ask and answer large questions.

Here's an example. The following interesting question occurs to you. "If a poor, basically decent man, caught up in the egotism of youth and holding to the twin ideas that the end justifies the means and that great individuals can step outside the law, decides to steal some money and commits a murder in the process, will he stick to his so-to-speak principles and consider himself justified in his actions or will his conscience cause him to confess, leading to his ultimate redemption?" This of course is the question Dostoyevsky poses and answers in *Crime and Punishment.*

It is an excellent question. But we have to wonder if Raskolnikov's conscience would work so admirably in real life that he'd confess and willingly let himself be shipped off to Siberia. How many confessions of that sort have you heard of? I can't think of any. It appears that Dostoyevsky wants to answer his question in a certain way, even if it isn't the truest way, because he is arguing for the existence of God, the power of God's love, and the possibility of human goodness. The novel is great, but it isn't a true inquiry; the fix is in. Whatever Raskolnikov would do in real life, in *Crime and Punishment* he *will* confess and he *will* find God. That is Dostoyevsky's agenda.

> My father pointed to the moon and asked me what color it was. I couldn't tell. So he told me to look at the horizon and then glance back quickly at the moon. Then I saw it: it was pale green!
>
> — ALDEN BAKER

Take a second example, where a question and answer both occur to you in rapid succession. The following question pops into your head: "What would a book about creativity for children focus on?" An answer immediately arrives: "Such a book should focus on giving children permission to make mistakes. Maybe it could be called *101 Mistakes Every Child Should Make.*" But when you sit down to write it, you discover that focusing entirely on making mistakes, no matter how cleverly you maintain that focus, is too negative and one-sided an approach. Part of you still wants to provide the answer you first arrived at, because it's an important one, but part of you recognizes that a new answer is needed, one that is more rounded and complete. Do you stick with the first answer or surrender to the need to find the second? In this example my hunch is that surrendering to a new answer is the better path. But whichever path you choose, you're likely to experience anxiety and self-doubt in the process.

> *I'd asked ten or fifteen people for suggestions. Finally one lady friend asked the right question. "Well, what do you love most?" That's how I started painting money.*
>
> — ANDY WARHOL

You may wonder why I suggested that you engage in this two-step process and then focused on the problems inherent in the process. I did so because I wanted you to respect the complexities of the work we do. At the same time, I wanted to remind you that despite these difficulties we can still end up with something as fine as *Crime and Punishment* or as useful as your book on creativity for children. This two-step process—asking yourself an interesting question, then trying to answer it—only sounds easy, but for all its hardness it can result in the best work human beings are capable of producing.

EXERCISE 26 • *Ask One Question*

What makes for an *interesting* question? Today, begin to develop your criteria for deciding which questions are interesting and which aren't really. Must a question never have been posed before? Or never answered adequately? Must it have great inherent difficulty, so that you really get to sweat as you try to answer it? Or must it be a question whose answer helps people live better lives?

Tomorrow, pose yourself some interesting questions. Make a long list of them. Take your time and then select one to answer, or let it select you.

The day after tomorrow, visit with your question, have tea with it, take it out to lunch. If the desire to answer it wells up in you, then you will have a new creative project on your hands.

27. Have Feathers Handy

Certainly you could sit in a bare room and create. Monks in their unadorned cells have painted icons and illustrated manuscripts, prisoners have written novels and poetry, ascetics with few worldly possessions have produced revolutionary philosophies and inventions. You don't need to be surrounded by stimuli or have the best tools in order to create. Tools are useful and sometimes vital and the objects with which we surround ourselves can, like the stained-glass windows of a church, filter reality beautifully and move us mysteriously. But no paintbrush, sunrise, or nude model ever made a painter.

Indeed, it often seems as if people are harmed by accumulating too many tools. One of my clients had a studio full of instruments: a dozen synthesizers, scores of drums from around the world, and reed instruments of every description, in clay, bamboo, ebony, you name it. But it had been many years since he'd done any composing. Another client, a would-be writer, purchased every new writing book that came out. But still she never wrote. Owning the tools of your trade does not guarantee that you'll create; and if those tools sit around unused for too long, they only become a reproach.

But whereas too many tools may prove stifling, keeping resonant objects nearby can ignite your creativity. A postcard on my desk of the Place des Vosges in Paris always puts me in a creative mood. So does a painting of irises on the mantle, done by my daughter Kira when she was thirteen and studying van Gogh. Then there are the odd books I've accumulated—on Los Angeles painters, chaos theory, the Soviet short story, neurophilosophy—my CDs of Andean music and the Indigo Girls, a certain rusted iron gecko, a wooden African spoon, and a tailless clay horse: each of these objects in its own mysterious way supports my creativity.

> *I like to have rope, jute, feathers, even driftwood on hand to study. Then things begin to happen—mentally.*
> — HORATHEL HALL

How do I actually make use of these things? I don't know. But when you have resonant objects nearby, they work wonders. With some feathers handy, you have a talisman of every bird that ever took flight. When you have pebbles on your coffee table, you have the tallest mountain ranges right beside you. Maybe a feather will find its way into your next collage, or maybe its job is to add lightness to your next poem. Maybe the books on your shelf are there for actual reference, or maybe they're there to remind you of Byzantine libraries and ideas that never die. Sometimes these supportive objects have some direct use, but just as often their job is to stir us and join us on our journey of exploration.

EXERCISE **27** • *Gather Some Objects*

Let's say that you mean to paint a red painting, because red somehow has been on your mind lately. In that case, gather some red things: a poster of Matisse's painting *The Artist and His Family,* five or six varieties of apples, red candies, whipped cream mixed with red food coloring, a brick, a Chinese red vase, an apple-and-cinnamon scented red candle, a lock of hair from a redheaded friend. Put the Matisse poster on a table, anchor it with apples, and use it as a giant red place mat to hold your other red delicacies.

Wherever I go, I collect sand.
— CONNIE ZEHR

Or let's say that you mean to learn to cook Indian food. Instead of adding another cookbook to your collection, find an Indian market and purchase some spices. Buy black mustard seeds, cumin seeds, cinnamon sticks, cardamom pods, a lump of asafetida, and anything else that catches your fancy, including that package of edible gold foil, even though you haven't a clue what to do with them. At home, put each spice in a bowl and visit with them. Aren't black mustard seeds amazingly tiny? You could put thousands of them in a thimble. And the gold foil . . . has anyone ever made a gold foil sandwich? Roast some cumin seeds, grind them up, enjoy their aroma.

Or let's say that you're a federal prosecutor hoping to write a book about your prosecution of a corrupt federal judge. Gather on a large table some relevant objects: a photograph of the defendant, a copy of your summation to the jury, the tie you wore on the day the verdict was returned, the menu from the restaurant where you ate lunch throughout the trial, handwritten letters from the witness whom you befriended, a coaster from the bar where you sometimes drank with FBI agents. These objects will do you more good than a stack of Grisham novels or how-to books on plotting. They'll jog your memory, which will be good for your story, and they'll remind you that you served justice well, which will be good for your soul.

28. Carve Basalt

One of the great impediments to unleashing our creativity is the fear that we're not equal to creative and intellectual tasks. The stone in front of us, which we would love to transform into the face of a girl, looks too obdurate, too hard to carve, too much like a stone and too little like a face. We have the sure sense that our first gouge will ruin everything, that we'll waste the stone and disappoint ourselves. So we back off.

I'd never seen basalt before, that volcanic stone the pre-Columbians carved in. I kept looking at it out in the Rio Grande, wondering if I could carve it.
— SHIRLEY STARK

This sense that the work is too hard, that any attempt to think big and tackle mighty themes will inevitably lead to failure, haunts songwriters, sculptors, sociologists, and microbiologists alike. You try to write pop songs rather than deep songs, bore yourself in the process, get blocked, and write nothing. You sculpt shapes you can manage rather than shapes you would love to try. You repeat the same sociological experiment for two decades, refining it and mastering it, because you fear venturing into territory where you might look a fool. You gain expert knowledge of one amino acid, get grants to study it, and earn a reputation, but don't allow yourself to leap intellectually. Creators in every field stifle their own creativity by announcing to themselves, "Doing *that* would be far too hard."

A singer-songwriter calls me from New York about once a month. She's very young, not even twenty-five, but she feels old, especially for rock and roll. She hates her day job, she can't shake her depression, and, although people say they love the sound of her voice, she passes up most singing opportunities.

She also isn't writing songs. To her, writing a song feels as difficult as scaling Mt. Everest. The very thought of writing a song daunts and defeats her. Of course her problem has nothing to do with songwriting per se; her problem is the secret muffled message she sends herself about the difficulty of creating and the smallness of her ability. That message completely enjoins her from trying. What really distinguishes the productive artist from the would-be artist? The former looks at the blank ceiling of the Sistine Chapel and says, "Hm, I wonder what should go there?" The other says, "My God, no way I'm touching that!"

> *I made my first trip west of the Hudson and it was a revelation. The naked musculature of the Rockies was overpowering and my painting responded.*
>
> — ELAINE DE KOONING

Most people are in the second category. They see difficulty where the creative person sees opportunity. If you find yourself in that second category, what should you do? First, become aware of that secret muffled message. Second, when you hear it, try to change it. In cognitive therapy this technique is called "thought substitution." You could try replacing "This is too hard" with one of the following messages:

- "This will be easy"
- "This will be hard but not *that* hard"
- "This will be *very* hard, but I'm game"

Each of these three affirmations has its merits, and it doesn't matter which one you choose. What's important is that you dispel the idea that creating is too hard, that it's somehow beyond your capabilities. In this period of exploration, it would be good if you got acquainted with using all three of these affirmations. Let's practice doing that.

EXERCISE **28** • *Tackle a Really Hard Project*

Today, pick a very hard creative project, one that you would not normally contemplate even for an instant. Instead of writing a song, start writing a musical. Instead of writing a book, begin work on a twelve-volume series. Say to yourself, "This will be easy." Think and feel that it will be easy. Begin.

Tomorrow, continue with this very hard project. Having worked on it for a day, you now have some idea just how easy and just how hard it will be. Say, "This will be hard, but not *that* hard." Continue working.

The day after tomorrow, with two days of work under your belt, you can better evaluate your project's hardness. Maybe the idea of writing a musical now really excites you, and maybe two of the songs have already gotten written. But maybe you also see a thousand problems ahead. Say "This will be *very* hard, but I'm game." Just continue.

At the end of these three days, take a moment to determine which phrase you like the best. Then remember to use it. When you come upon a blank Sistine Chapel ceiling posted with the notice "Paint me," instead of exclaiming "This is too hard!" remember your affirmation. Then gulp and get out your paintbrush.

29. Abstract Everything

The human animal has it built right into her to love both the literal and the figurative, the concrete and the symbolic. As the Almond Joy/Mounds jingle has it, "Sometimes you feel like a nut, sometimes you don't." One day you want your elm trees to look not only like elms but precisely like your elms, so that anyone encountering your painting will be forced to exclaim, "Those are Jane's elms!" But the very next day you slash at your canvas with purples and golds to capture the feeling provoked by the elm out your window, in the process producing something that no one can identify as your elm or anyone else's.

In past times when one lived in contact with nature, abstraction was easy; it was done unconsciously. Now in our denaturalized age abstraction becomes an effort.

— PIET MONDRIAN

Still, each of us tends to gravitate toward one or the other way of thinking, toward a taste for the literal or a taste for abstraction. When my students first start writing their experiential learning essays, many have terrible trouble providing concrete examples to support their abstract generalizations. Others have a hard time abstracting principles, rules, and generalizations from their concrete experiences. Some want to talk about elm-ness without showing a single branch or leaf; others want to focus on particular elms without discussing what it means to be a tree. It takes weeks before everyone in the class manages to get both elm-ness and the particulars of elms into their papers.

This week, our fifteenth together, I'd like you to think deeply about abstraction. Abstraction is itself an abstract word and has no single meaning. Sometimes it means "a process by which we get at the essence of things." Mondrian once said that, like any painter, he believed in the reality of a flower, but that he was looking for a deeper reality hidden within: he was searching for the very essence of the flower. In the process of abstracting you learn what all members of a class—all winged creatures, all flowers, all protons, all Democrats—have in common. When you reach that point, you can render the flight of birds with a single gesture or arrive at exactly the right phrase to describe the Democratic presidential candidate in your novel. Given the great value of such results, it's natural that creators fall in love with abstraction.

> *Abstraction is real, probably more real than nature. I prefer to see with closed eyes.*
> — JOSEF ALBERS

Abstraction is also the process by which we represent things. Every word in our language is abstract, because it represents something else. "Blue" is not blue, it represents blue. "Love" is not love itself and "is" hasn't more is-ness than any other word. The sign of the cross is an abstraction and a representation: with a single gesture something about a believer's sense of devotion and about Christ's ordeal are communicated. If you tinkered with that gesture, as an artist might for the sake of her film or painting, you'd be creating a different abstract idea and representing something new—something that might well make Christians angry.

An everyday creative person is intrigued by abstraction in both these senses—as a means to get at the essence of things, and as the central way we communicate—and uses what she learns to make her stories leaner and more elemental, to add texture to her photographs by employing images with multiple meanings, to find the central connection between the indigenous people she studied in New Guinea and the one she examined in Peru. An everyday creative person trains herself to fathom the power and meaning of abstractions.

EXERCISE **29** • *Render an Object Abstractly*

Take a book of Piet Mondrian's art out of the library. Make sure that it's one that details his process of abstracting from the natural world. Notice that he first selects a subject—say, an apple tree—and draws it naturalistically. His next sketch is more abstract, but you can still recognize the apple tree without straining. Little by little and sketch by sketch, the apple tree disappears, and what is left is Mondrian's understanding of the essence of apple trees, rendered fully abstractly.

Even if you don't consider yourself a visual artist, do the same thing. Choose an object that interests you—a curled cat, a factory smokestack, a French vase. First try to draw it realistically, getting down every whisker, brick, or design element. Then progressively draw the object more abstractly, leaving out more details with each subsequent drawing. Try not to leap from the realistic image to the abstract one, but rather get there step by step via many intermediate drawings. When you're done, just murmur the word "abstraction." Let the word sink in. Learn to love it.

30. Reinvent the Wheel

Creative people make use of what's known but also feel compelled to reinvent the wheel, partly because they're skeptical about what they've been taught and partly because they find it thrilling to discover truths for themselves. Often their most creative work is prompted by the following sort of sudden thought: "Everybody says that 'x' is true, but is it? I wonder."

For instance, some researchers once wondered if psychiatrists really understood mental illness. They designed the following elegant experiment. They divided their subjects, practitioners in the mental health field, into two groups. A famous psychiatrist was enlisted to present to each group the same fictitious case study—of a perfectly sane middle-aged fellow, one with all the attributes we associate with good mental health, like an ability to form intimate relationships, a solid work history, and a record of volunteer activities.

To the first group, the psychiatrist ended his presentation by adding, "Now, isn't that about the healthiest person you've ever heard described?" To the second group he ended by adding, "Now, isn't that about the craziest person you've ever heard described?" Each group was then asked to rate the mental health of the individual portrayed in the vignette. The first group rated him healthy. The second group rated him crazy. Doesn't that boggle your mind? But the researchers were happy, because the results validated what they intuitively knew, that the psychiatric diagnostic process was neither science nor art but much more like a gentlemen's agreement.

If you sat placidly in graduate school, accepted the nostrums presented in your abnormal psychology classes, and left knowing how to use the American Psychological Association's diagnostic and statistical manual, you would have no trouble diagnosing patients, chatting with your peers about differential diagnoses, or accurately filling out insurance claims. But if pressed, you'd have to admit that you had no idea what mental illness really was, where it came from, what phenomena should be called abnormal (one year homosexuality is in, the next year homosexuality is out, all on a whim), what part nature, nurture, and culture played in producing the behaviors you saw, and, most important, what treatments helped your patients. You might even be forced to admit that your best bet would be to begin all over: to get rid of all labels and theories and see what a fresh start might bring to the business of insanity.

Almost all the horse sculptures I had ever seen had to do with giant war horses, invariably stallions, carrying generals off to kill people. Instead, I wanted to make a sculpture of a mare expecting a baby.

— DEBORAH BUTTERFIELD

To some people it is unnerving to learn that a whole field of study can be built on quicksand. But an everyday creative person is actually pleased. He's pleased that his intuitive sense of what's true and what's false is accurate, and pleased that knowledge is far from a finished enterprise. If knowledge were finished, what would he study? On a regular basis an everyday creative person must start from the very beginning, from ground zero, because what passes for the best knowledge, even though vouched for by all the experts, is entirely inaccurate.

There are many reasons to reinvent the wheel and many occasions when doing so is the only honorable course. But most people are afraid to think this way. They fear learning that what they believe to be true perhaps isn't. Too much is put at risk by such revelations. But I hope you'll accept these risks and count yourself among those who willingly reinvent the wheel, simply because the truth and your own progress demand it.

> *The prospect of a sympathetic rediscovery of the horse within the art of my own time was an exciting one. Could Rosa Bonheur find happiness with Andy Warhol?*
> — RICHARD MCLEAN

EXERCISE 30 • *Roll a Wheel*

Get a wheel, any kind. A wheel from a toy truck would be a good choice, since you're going to keep it on your desk next to your pen holder.

Whenever you start a new creative project, take the wheel off your desk and roll it across the floor. Watch it slow down and keel over. Return it to its ceremonial place and murmur to yourself, "If a wheel needs reinventing, I'm ready."

Consider your current work. Is it languishing half done for no reason you can name? Go back to the beginning, to your original vision, and reconnect with that first idea. Or what about your career? Is it stalled? Reconsider what you love about your work and how you could revitalize it in some elemental way. Don't fear starting fresh. Sometimes a fresh start is the *only* answer.

31. Innovate

The automobile, the atomic bomb, and the Internet are large-scale innovations, but my mother's latest composed salad, made up of baby spinach leaves, chopped celery, and Greek olives, is an innovation for her. At ninety she is still innovating, because she is still interested in life and still adamant about making healthy, tasty food.

> *I work with nature, although in completely new terms. For me nature is not landscape, but the dynamism of visual forces.*
> — BRIDGET RILEY

Sometimes you consciously decide to aim for the new. You feel stale and you say to yourself, "I have to go someplace I've never been before or die of boredom." The next week you find yourself sitting in a coffee house in Shinjuku, a Tokyo neighborhood. Maybe you say to yourself "I need a new subject to paint" or "My business needs a new product if we're going to compete successfully." Maybe you buy every mousetrap on the market but none do the trick, so you say to yourself "I must find something new," research mousetraps, and discover that mice have allergies, which gets you thinking. In each of these cases you are consciously on the lookout for something new.

Then there are innovations that happen because you've been seeking an answer and stumble upon it through fortunate accident. For years a certain biologist was looking for an enzyme that would destroy chicken feathers naturally, so as to help chicken growers with one of their biggest waste problems. One day he noticed that the feathers in a particular spot beneath a neighbor's chicken coop had vanished. Because something wasn't there that should have been there, he made the discovery that had eluded him up until that moment.

Other innovations come out of the blue. As a baggage handler, you notice that the baggage of first-class customers, whose luggage is boarded first, is the last to come out of the plane. This makes you wonder if it isn't poor policy to have the customers who pay the most wait the longest for their luggage. Your observation comes out

> *I have never been able to understand the artist whose image never changes.*
> — LEE KRASNER

of the blue and connects to nothing you'd been thinking about previously, but in no time your innovation—that first-class luggage be boarded last, so as to come off first—becomes an industry standard.

New things occur in these three ways. First, we actively seek them out and are fortunate to discover them quickly. Second, we seek them out and they elude us, but when a serendipitous accident occurs we're prepared for it and make our discovery. Third, they just happen out of the blue, by virtue of the fact that we're alert, open, and everyday creative. For an uncreative person nothing new ever happens, and she ends up believing that there's really nothing new under the sun. Her conservatism isn't a reflection of a desire to conserve what's good but rather a pessimistic surrender to a feeling that the past is all there is. She's against innovation for the odd reason that she just doesn't believe in it, even as the world around her changes daily.

An everyday creative person innovates. She innovates because she is thinking, and trains of thought inevitably lead to new destinations. She innovates because she has the desire to put her own fingerprints on every subject, so that her painting of sunflowers says something not said by van Gogh or anyone else. She innovates because she's hit a dead end but refuses to stay trapped there. She has so many reasons to innovate that if nothing new is stirring in her she stops everything to interrogate herself: "What's going on here? Am I trapped in a rut? Clinically depressed? I won't stand for it!"

EXERCISE 31 • *Innovate*

Your goal for the next few days is to aim for the new.

Today we'll start small. Do something you've always done but do it in a new way. Drive to work by a different route, buy a new brand of soft drink, change the color of the pens you use on your erasable boards. (I've recently taken to writing in pale green and pale yellow on one of my boards. I can barely read what I've written, but straining to make out my own notes is an interesting experience.)

Tomorrow, stretch a little. Change a procedure at work. Paint in the dark. Imagine yourself as a leopard during dance class. Write your boss a memo proposing that everyone work from home on Fridays during the summer.

The day after tomorrow, stretch farther. Start on a new project, a *radically* new project, one so new that it frightens you. If you've always written magazine articles, start a novel. If you've always written poetry, start an essay. Do what's frighteningly different, if just for one day.

32. Leave for the Unknown

We're at the end of the time I've set aside for exploration. But of course, everyday creative people never stop exploring. This section is a new exploration for me and the next fifty-seven sections will be new explorations, too. Then, when this book is done, I'll hunt for the headwaters

Be brave, right through, and leave for the unknown.

— RABINDRANATH TAGORE

of some other unexplored river. I hope to go on traipsing into the unknown until a greater unknown takes me away and cuts short my earthly explorations.

A certain image helps me remember why people find it so difficult to create. I see two plateaus separated by a deep gorge hardly three feet wide at its narrowest point. The near plateau, where a would-be creator lives, is barren, while the far plateau is jungle-covered, wild, and mysterious. Every day the would-be creator walks right up to the edge of his plateau, stares into the gorge to its floor two hundred feet below, and says to himself, "If I try to get across I'll fall and kill myself." Then he glances across at the tangled vines that obscure the jungle interior, making it impossible to know what riches or dangers are hidden there, and murmurs to himself, "Even if I did manage to get across, something bad would happen."

He is aware that his side of the gorge is barren. But he's afraid of that short leap and afraid of the jungle interior. His instinct for survival, his fear of the unknown, or some elemental human inertia causes him to stay put, even though he is perfectly aware that his current life is unrewarding. To think that clay, pigments, words, or ideas could put one in the same such fear! Yet would-be creators of all kinds pace on their plateaus, held in check by fear of that small leap and that unknown territory—even though the dangers are largely chimerical.

The psychologist Otto Rank, who took a special interest in artists, likened them to heroes. We know that everyday creative people are very fallible, very human, and regularly unheroic, just like you and me, so to call them heroic feels like hyperbole. Yet, since so many people fear making a creative effort, it turns out that there must *be* something heroic about launching yourself across that gorge and into that unknown jungle. Maybe everyday creative people really are heroic and maybe the courage they show is among the most important: the courage to leave for the unknown.

> *Make voyages!*
> *Attempt them . . .*
> *there's nothing else.*
> — TENNESSEE WILLIAMS

Besides, some of the dangers may be real. Maybe it is dangerous to get too involved with color: won't life look drab when you return from your painting explorations? Maybe it is dangerous to obsess about language: how will the bills get paid if you spend your days writing poetry? Maybe it is dangerous to commit to composing: what if the music you compose is jarring and sends audiences scattering? Maybe the psychological and practical dangers of leaving for the unknown are real enough that we have further reason to call creative people heroic.

We are built to explore but we are also built to avoid exploration. We are genetically coded for both. In order to leave for the unknown on a regular basis—that is, to go wherever our creative efforts want to lead us—it looks like we need to have regular chats with ourselves about why that's worth doing, given the chimerical and actual dangers. The reasons to create are plentiful, but still we have to convince ourselves to take that leap and to venture into the dark territory of the unfamiliar.

EXERCISE 32 • *Make a List and Have a Chat*

Spend some time today listing the reasons why it's important to venture into the unknown. My partial list would include:

- Because life would be too dull if I didn't
- Because that way I can have vicarious adventures
- Because what I come back with has proven useful to others
- Because what I learn there I can't learn anywhere else

Tomorrow, have a chat with yourself. Set up two chairs so that they face each other. Sit in the first chair and begin arguing against venturing into the unknown. "When I sit and think for too long I get anxious." Move to the other chair and respond. "Yes, but that just means that I should work on my nerves. Am I going to let anxiety prevent me from creating?" Return to the first chair and counter your counterargument. Engage in a real dialogue.

My clients find this "chair work" both scary and transformative. See if you can stick out the dialogue until you've convinced yourself that leaving for the unknown makes great sense—so much sense that you bound right off, over the chasm and into the jungle.

PART 5

Go Deep

Weeks 17-20

33. Dive

What makes deep-sea diving dangerous? You could lose your way in the underwater darkness. You could puncture your air hose on a sharp rock outcropping. You could be attacked by a shark. You could stay down too long, mesmerized by the sights, and run out of air. You could rise to the surface too quickly and get the bends. And this is the partial list.

> I love all men who dive. Any fish can swim near the surface, but it takes a great whale to go downstairs five miles or more.
>
> — HERMAN MELVILLE

"Going deep" as a creator means taking equivalent risks. You risk asking the sorts of questions that demand intense concentration and iron discipline to answer. You risk spending two years on a novel that never ignites. You risk admitting to yourself that you haven't a clue how to realize the sculpture you began so optimistically. You risk confronting your own demons and shortcomings. Which are the greater risks? I wouldn't assume that the deep-sea diver has the harder time of it.

The novelist Arthur Golden wrote the first draft of *Memoirs of a Geisha* in the third person. But it didn't work. He hadn't penetrated the main character's skin or illuminated her universe. So, although it would cost him a great deal more time and effort, he took the risk he felt he had to take and rewrote his novel in the first person. He tried to enter the geisha's mind and body, to become her. If Sayuri is a success, it is because Golden risked throwing good time after bad and devoting himself to entirely re-visioning his novel.

As with deep-sea diving, when we create we can lose our bearings in the murky depths. We can miss what we're looking for—even a whole shipwrecked ocean liner—because of darkness. We can lose oxygen or fear losing it and precipitate a deadly anxiety attack. All of these dangers are waiting.

> *The task is to go as deeply as possible into the darkness.*
> — ANTHEA FRANCINE

But if we try to stay near the surface, where the sunlight penetrates and guides us, we will never see the glories that exist down below. We'll have to rely on others to tell us about them. Those people will create—and we'll envy them. Isn't it wiser to take even serious risks, so as to explore where the fish are phosphorescent?

Creators are continuously confronted by darkness. That's where all their new work resides. That darkness is real—and can be really discouraging. The novelist E. L. Doctorow once explained that "writing a novel is like driving at night. You can only see as far as your headlights allow, but you can make the whole trip that way." Doctorow's metaphor has quite an encouraging ring to it. But far too often our headlights aren't working. Far too often we have to drive blind, somehow intuiting where the road is even though we can't see a bit of it. No wonder so many would-be writers stay in the garage with the light on!

The truth is that you must proceed blind and uncertain. You will run into many dead ends. You will run off the road and sometimes crash badly. But you can't let the darkness stop you. Whether you envision an inky opaqueness like the depths of the sea or an icy blackness like a moonless night in the desert, some vast darkness does await you. You must proceed through it, with only a little light to guide you or with no light at all. Maybe you'll even find the darkness inviting. For out there, somewhere, are all your future accomplishments.

EXERCISE **33A** • *Dive*

It's time for you to do a little diving.

Get ten sheets of paper. Pick a subject that allows you to go deep, like friendship, desire, madness, revenge, intuition. Think about your subject. Then, on the first sheet of paper, write down an answer to the question, "What are my deepest thoughts about friendship (or whatever you've chosen)?" When you're done, turn that sheet over.

A new blank sheet is waiting. As you stare at that second white sheet, ask yourself, "Can I go deeper?" Try to maintain a sense that you're heading for some elemental bottom. Write as much or as little as you like. When you're done, turn that second sheet over.

Do the same with sheets three through ten, each time asking yourself, "Can I go deeper?" Maybe what you'll write on that last sheet is "Don't know." That's possible. That's certainly the risk we take when we go deep. But maybe you'll discover something really noteworthy about friendship or madness or intuition. That, too, is a possible outcome!

Dry off now. But dive again tomorrow—maybe deep into your current creative project.

WEEK 17

34. Buy Bewilderment

No one likes to feel bewildered. I don't and I'm sure you don't either. But disliking that feeling and avoiding it at all costs are two different things.

An everyday creative person makes an effort to embrace bewilderment, even though she dislikes the feeling, because she knows that she has no other good choice. Every creative journey is marked by patches and even long stretches of bewilderment as, disoriented

Sell your cleverness and buy bewilderment.

— JALAL RUMI

and upset, you realize that you don't know what to do next. These patches of not knowing just can't be avoided, unless you refuse to create.

What do people do when they don't know what to do next and want to rid themselves of that bad feeling? They may do something easy, like quote an expert. They may do something clever, like make a brilliant distinction which says nothing. They may do something deceitful, like argue for a theory they've hardly thought through yet. These and many other shortcuts are traps to avoid, because they prevent us from really using our potential and creating deeply.

Try to embrace bewilderment instead. This may mean that the book you thought you were writing about your father must be about your mother instead, as bewildering as that seems. It may mean that your current painting style has run its course and that you have a great, new darkness to enter. It may mean that you're on the verge of a breakthrough that can only occur if you let out a real shriek: "I have no idea what I'm doing!" When you feel bewildered, don't look for ways to rid yourself of the feeling. Just go forward.

I write this book in the mornings. Afternoons I'm working on a book called *Sleep Thinking,* in which I outline a program for reducing stress, solving problems, and increasing creativity while you sleep. I don't know what will go into that book, which makes it a bewildering project to contemplate. All I know is its central truth, that when we invite our brain to work at night we sleep more soundly and live more vitally. I know this from my own experience and from my work with clients. I have the intuition that I have something important to communicate. But nothing else about that book is known to me right now.

> *You know it's very hard to maintain a theory in the face of life that comes crashing about you.*
>
> — ALICE NEEL

I have no statistics, studies, or questionnaire responses to build the book around. I have nothing but the central idea. I think that most people in this situation would feel that they weren't ready to begin writing. First they'd want to get a degree in sleep studies or interview a few experts. It would cross their mind to collaborate with a dream expert or a whole team of specialists. In short, they would want to know before beginning. Research has its place, but my primary job is to access what I know already and not rely on what others have to say. I need to accept that my most important researches are interior ones.

EXERCISE **34A** • *Face Not Knowing*

Contemplate something that you're certain you don't understand. Let's say that it's the engine of your car. Go into the garage, turn on the light, and lift up the hood of your car. What do you see? An array of completely meaningless gizmos. Notice the feeling in the pit of your stomach. That's anxiety. Notice your thoughts. "I could never figure this out in a million years!" Notice what your feet want to do. They want to run. Bewilderment is setting in.

Now, consciously switch your thoughts. Say, "I don't understand what I see here, but I don't need to feel frightened." Stand up a little straighter. Work to breathe normally. Say, "What a bewildering thing an engine is." Accept that you don't know how your car's engine works, but imagine that you could learn.

After a while your stomach will begin to settle and your vision will clear. You might even be tempted to reach down and unscrew a cap or two. Store away this feeling.

EXERCISE **34B** • *Buy Bewilderment*

The following phrases are virtually synonymous. Pick the one you like the best and repeat it like a mantra every day, many times a day.

- "I buy bewilderment willingly"
- "It's all right not to know"
- "I can enter the chaos and create there"
- "I am prepared to work blind"
- "I can move forward without a destination"
- "What I need is inside the darkness"
- "I would love things to be easy, but I prefer truthfulness"
- "To create, I must embrace bewilderment"

WEEK 18

35. Parachute into Enemy Territory

Do you feel particularly alert? Is your adrenaline flowing? Are your senses functioning at their highest pitch? Probably not. Usually we only fully wake up in a system-wide way when we find ourselves in an alarm situation, facing a life-threatening emergency. We are built to nurse our resources so that when our child is pinned under a car we can muster the extraordinary strength necessary to lift up the car's front end and save him. We don't have that strength when it comes to opening a jar. Our genes have made a choice, that running on all cylinders must be an occasional affair or else we'll burn our motor out.

> *To become conscious of what one is doing to earn his feeling of heroism is the main self-analytic problem of life.*
>
> — ERNEST BECKER

But deeply creating requires more adrenaline than we ordinarily expend. Our senses need to be functioning, our brain cells need to be engaged, our whole body needs to be present. In order for this to happen, we need to feel as if our work is not only important but even vitally important, as important as getting our child out from under that car. Our ability to go deep relates to our feelings about the work we undertake: that doing it is a life-and-death affair and that our life has acquired the quality of a mission.

Consider the following scenario. A civilian, enlisted by the military because of his special skills, must parachute into Nazi Germany, learn an important secret, and get that information back to the Allies. He'll have to live by his wits, kill or be killed, and treat everyone, even his contacts, as possible betrayers. Nor is he likely to get out alive; this is surely a suicide mission. How many times have we seen variations of this plot played out on the silver screen? Yet each time we're stirred by it.

What exactly is so powerful about this plot line? It's not simply that we have an interest in the spy's success. It turns out that we love such movies even when the hero is a German spy parachuted into England to kill Churchill. What really stirs us is the fact that this spy is on a mission of vital importance to a whole nation. The future of his country and even the world hang in the balance. We crave the chance to live in such a heightened fashion, doing something equally important, and we identify with that spy no matter what country he happens to be helping.

An everyday creative person lives with the intensity of that spy. You too can have that feeling of supreme aliveness, just by tackling a mighty creative project. You can feel that alert, intense, and engaged. Is this one of those rainy afternoons with nothing much happening? Are you feeling dull and pointless? In an instant you can initiate a life-and-death struggle, just by saying to yourself "My work is vital. I must create."

Not to dare is to lose oneself.
— SØREN KIERKEGAARD

People who live this way have to be careful. The mind and the body need breaks from such intensity. Maybe three hours of creating will exhaust you. Then nap—just like soldiers nap in combat, at the drop of a hat and even standing up. Maybe a year of thinking hard about your scientific theory will melt your brain. Then back away from the fire and get off the front lines, as firefighters must who battle a raging forest fire for too long. Take all the necessary precautions. But live intensely and dangerously. The world may not depend on your efforts, but you do.

EXERCISE 35 • *Parachute into Enemy Territory*

Imagine that you're a spy who's been parachuted into enemy territory. Really picture it. Feel yourself plummeting down through the night air, then through the branches of a towering pine. Feel yourself hitting the ground, banging up your knees, maybe cracking a rib. Despite the pain, you have to get right up and hide your parachute. Suddenly you hear a noise. Are you undone already? You reach for your pistol. But it's just a deer. You sigh deeply, the deepest sigh of your life. Now what? You're in the middle of a pine forest in enemy territory and you can't see two feet in any direction.

Play out this plot. Get to a nearby village. Find your contact, the old professor. Measure your every move. Jump when the professor's phone rings and hear how suspicious he sounds, whispering on the phone. Should you stay or should you run? The fate of the free world hangs in the balance. No, you don't trust him. You'd better run! Now you're outside and the dogs are barking.

The next time you create, bring these feelings with you: that what you are doing is vital, that you are making a difference, that you are fully alert, and that despite the dangers you can create beautifully.

WEEK 18

36. Get Unacademic

There's that well-known adage, "Those who can, do, and those who can't, teach." It's unfair to tar all teachers with this broadbrush criticism. But while many teachers do make a positive difference in the lives of their students, we also know from our own experience that few classes are really interesting and few teachers really inspiring. Like you, I've suffered through many boring classes and encountered many uncreative teachers.

The happiest face to put on this is to say that an everyday creative person somehow survives school and goes on to create anyway. She stubbornly determines not to let her vitality be killed off by mean-spirited Mrs. O'Grady, her third-grade teacher, or by her psychology professor in her freshman year who defined tenure as "Gone fishing." When she encounters a lively teacher who encourages her to go deep she rejoices, and when she encounters an ill-prepared or small-minded teacher she makes faces, acts out, rebels, drinks ink, and drowns him out with hoots and catcalls. Or maybe she just keeps quiet—but what she says to herself is, "I won't let this professor murder my creative nature."

> *Let a student enter art school with this advice: no matter how good the school is, his education is in his own hands. All education must be self-education.*
> — ROBERT HENRI

A lot of harm can be done in school and many of us must actively reclaim our curiosity and our creativity after fifteen or twenty years of being educated. We have to learn to combine ideas across disciplines and recognize that disparate subjects—like art and biology, say—may reside in different buildings on campus but connect in real life. We must learn, in short, that our job is to overcome the limitations of a contemporary education. For we do want to be educated; we do want our minds stretched; we do want to learn about and be thrilled by what's gone on before us.

Where will our creative education come from, if not from school? It will come primarily from our own studies, from following our own interests, and from doing our own work. The last avenue is the most important of all. We learn how to write songs by writing them. We learn how to draw by drawing. We learn how to invent by inventing. If we think that, having gone to school for so many years, having even gone to schools that purported to teach us about painting, writing, or composing, we should already know how to create, then when we find our creative efforts dramatically uneven we'll tend to disparage ourselves and feel blocked.

The truth is that we do not know how to do anything until we do it. Sometimes we don't know how to do it for years on end, but during those years of writing our first novel or barging down a dead-end road trying to solve a recalcitrant math puzzle, we are educating ourselves. The only good education is our own experience.

Schools and things that painters taught me kept me from painting as I wanted to. I decided that I was a very stupid fool not to say what I wanted to say when I painted.

— GEORGIA O'KEEFFE

Each of us walks into a new class for the first time like van Gogh arriving at his first portrait class: hopeful, attentive, open, curious. We arrive dying to learn. Van Gogh listened to his famous teacher, saw what the other students were painting, and went ballistic, so unlifelike did their portraits look. He could do nothing but paint in his own way, violating all of his well-respected teacher's instructions. The teacher yelled at him. The other students winced. Van Gogh fled and never returned. He needed just one day of portrait class to realize that his painting education would have to come from his own studies and not from teachers.

EXERCISE **36** • *Shred a Textbook*

Buy a used or (if you feel extravagant) new textbook. Or use one left over from your college days. A cell biology text from ten years ago would be a good choice, or any text on the philosophy of art, the psychology of art, or aesthetics. A grammar text would work especially well; choose one with lots of rules that make you feel stupid. Whatever book you choose, go to town on it, ripping and shredding. Yes, you may be tearing up some insights and good information. But you're also reminding yourself in a visceral way that your best education comes from personal experience, not from academia.

Because I'd like you to have a visceral experience, please don't use an electric shredder. Rip out each page by hand, really enjoying the ripping. Rip them out by twos, threes, and fours, then rip them right down the middle, where the columns divide, or crosswise, right through the captions. Rip them this way and that, creating torn pieces like birds' beaks and half lizards. A nice flourish would be to make textbook confetti—you don't have to make it too fine—to use in a ceremony that celebrates your vow to lead, not follow.

WEEK 19

37. Put Up a Big Idea

We are bombarded with minutia—mail soliciting our car insurance and life insurance dollars, phone calls about changing our phone service and subscribing to the local newspaper, television coverage of the weekend grosses of the latest movies, hundreds of details at work, Internet information about everything under the sun, and our own racing, disconnected thoughts. In this onslaught, the big ideas that really matter can easily get lost. One way to help prevent such losses is to write a big idea on your erasable board and leave it there for a long time, for weeks and even months, to remind you of the central theme of your current work or to help you incubate a new project. When an idea is up on your board like this, it holds special weight and garners special attention.

It's best that you put your big idea up in extra-large letters, so that it really stands out. It's also wise to keep it to a single word or a short phrase. "Freedom of speech," "color," "crazy family," "voodoo economics," or "volume" are the kinds of words and phrases I have in mind. Take "color," for example. A physicist interested in color would focus on the properties of light. A biologist would focus on the way the eye and the brain process color information. An art historian would focus on the twentieth century color revolution precipitated by the Post Expressionists and the Fauves. But ideas cross the artificial boundaries that get erected between disciplines, and so an everyday creative person is interested in *all* of this. He reminds himself of the breadth and depth of his interest by putting up a single word:

Ideas are the root of creation.
— ERNEST DIMNET

Color

Don't worry about picking the perfect word or phrase. If you have a big idea in mind—say, finding ways to help elementary school teachers raise their students' consciousness about environmental issues—it doesn't much matter if the phrase you come up with is "earth awareness" or "eco-literacy." Either will do. The real tasks are arriving at a big idea to investigate and finding the resolve to pursue that idea wherever it takes you. If you manage those tasks, whatever phrase you choose to represent your idea will prove resonant.

You'll remember from our earlier discussion on

abstraction about the richness of idea words and phrases like "freedom of assembly," "love," "violence," or "momentum." When you place such a word or phrase up on your erasable board in big, bold letters and allow it to remain there, you'll begin to think more globally and more deeply. In fact, this process works so well that you might want to put a certain phrase up next to your computer. That phrase?

> *There is more dynamite in an idea than in many bombs.*
> — JOHN VINCENT

Everyday Creative

EXERCISE **37** • *Pick a Big Idea and Put It Up on Your Board*

What big idea would you like to wrestle with over the coming weeks and months? Most likely it's the one you're currently engaged on. In that case, just spend a few minutes finding the word or phrase that captures its depth, bigness, and richness. Once you've captured it, write it large on one of your erasable boards.

In preparation for writing a novel set in Los Angeles, you might put up the word:

City

In preparation for beginning a series of animal sculptures, you might put up the phrase:

Survival of the Fittest

In preparation for a new look at the global economy, you might put up the word:

Markets

In preparation for trying your hand at a novel that employs the device of magical realism, you might put up the word:

Superstition

In preparation for starting your nonfiction self-help book on stress management, you might put up the phrase:

Free-Floating Anxiety

If you don't have a current project underway or a big idea in mind, your task is to take the necessary time to find one. Once you do, corral a headline word or phrase and put it up in huge letters where you can't miss it.

WEEK 19

38. Get Nostalgic

Postmodernists, like the French philosopher Baudrillard, for example, know that the more sophisticated we become—as we pierce reality and see the void beyond—the more our sense of wonder is destroyed, along with our reasons for being. Once we understand who the Wizard is, how magical is Oz? Once we peek behind Disneyland's curtains, how swashbuckling are the Pirates of the Caribbean? When we genetically engineer life, what will life mean anyway? Deconstruction is great for the intellect, but it hurts the heart terribly.

We live in the present on shaky footing and it's

hard to create with the ground quivering beneath us. One way to recover our footing is through memory. The iciness of Italian snowcones from childhood, the tangerine look of summer sunlight at camp, the way our old bicycle's kickstand just never would work right—these are memories that ground us because they arise out

When the real is no longer what it used to be, nostalgia assumes its full meaning.
— JEAN BAUDRILLARD

of real experiences. One way to go deep creatively is to go back in memory. Nor could anything be easier: these memories aren't holed away in some library archive or rented storage space that requires us to take a special trip. They reside right here, within us. If you grow quiet and invite the past into the present, it will arrive.

It is good to remember the way we felt when we were awestruck by a classic novel at the age of twelve or how we were moved when we tiptoed outside to look at the full moon in a startlingly clear sky. It is excellent to remember our first loves and even our first frights—our firsts of all sorts—now that we have so many years of life experience and tend to feel things for the millionth time with only one millionth the intensity.

Nostalgia is a powerful emotion that reconnects us to the sweet and the bittersweet. We all possess a reservoir of special feelings about the toys and games of youth, the old smells and sights, the music of long-ago bands, the movies we grew up with. The naturalist who furthers our understanding of evolution is just a boy with a bug jar; the novelist who indicts her government is just a girl remembering that it wasn't right to pull her pigtails. Embedded in our best mature work are things from long ago that are just unforgettable, if only we remember them.

Nostalgia is part joy and part sadness. It's joyful to remember the way your mother smiled but painful to remember that she smiled so rarely and could murder you with her sarcasm. It's joyful to think back to the one time you got the gift you really wanted, but painful to remember the context, that usually you got presents that felt selected by strangers. Because nostalgia has sadness in it, you may want to avoid feeling it. But if you do, you miss out on much joy. You lose remembering what it was like rowing with a special friend. You lose what it was like at night during firefly season. You lose the taste of blueberry blintzes and pistachio ice cream. To spare yourself the bad memories, you lose the good memories. Maybe you must; maybe the bad is just too painful. But I hope not. I hope you can travel back and get nostalgic.

> *Remembrance is always now.*
> — GEORGE STEINER

EXERCISE 38 • *Get Nostalgic*

Start a nostalgia notebook.

Close your eyes and think back. Surrender to your own lived past. Let some bittersweet memory make itself felt. For me, right now, it's my crazy aunt Faye taking me to the movies, when I was six and she thirty, just before she was institutionalized for the rest of her life. We would take the bus to a wonderful block of theaters, halfway between my apartment house and the Bronx Zoo; a dozen theaters were arrayed there, six on either side of a grand avenue, all of them showing double features with shorts and cartoons included.

If I shift attention I'm at the Bronx Zoo, with its flamingos and its rock right at the entrance so that you could slide down it first thing upon entering and last thing before leaving. Then I'm at Coney Island, with its hot dog stands and cherry cheese knish aromas. Then I remember hot summer nights alive with kids' games and the smells of melted tar and the Atlantic Ocean. Then I see the girl I loved when I was thirteen: blonde and blue-eyed, she had just come from Israel and only spoke Hebrew.

Today, record a memory in your nostalgia notebook. Write about it for pages. Tomorrow, record another memory. Whenever you feel as if you've lost the past—and with it part of your creative legacy—return to your nostalgia notebook and do some remembering.

WEEK 20

39. Incubate

How do you incubate a creative project? It's neither as hard nor as mysterious as you might imagine, but it does require that you really *want* to support the growth of a new idea.

Paying regular attention to our budding ideas is rare. Why? For all the reasons I've described so far, having to do with our fear of making mistakes, our negative self-appraisals, our unwillingness to embrace the anxiety that comes with creating, our preening pride, our resistance to critical thinking—with, in short, our reluctance to become an everyday creative person.

If the sperm swam away from the egg, rather than toward it, we would have no word like incubation in our vocabulary. We'd also have no vocabulary and no species either. The same is true with creative work. If you push your thoughts away from you, no conception takes place and there is nothing to incubate. If you bottle up your creative urges, you've managed a perfect prophylactic maneuver. But if, on the other hand, you embrace your own ideas, then their growth naturally begins.

Wherever I go I need a period of incubation so that I may learn the essence of nature, which never wishes to be understood or yield herself.
— PAUL GAUGUIN

For instance, say that you wanted to write a self-help book—based on your experiences as an oncology nurse—that would help cancer patients cope with their chemotherapy and radiation treatments a little better. Given that most of us have a million things on our mind at any given time and given our reluctance to treasure our own ideas, you might not incubate your new book unless you:

- Began to wonder, "What advice would really help cancer patients? What do I want to offer them?"
- Said to yourself, "If I were teaching nursing students about working with cancer patients, what five (or ten or fifteen) things would I want them to know?"
- Put potential titles for and thoughts about your book up on your erasable board whenever a title or a thought struck you.
- Asked yourself each night before falling asleep, "How are you doing, book? Ready for me to begin writing?"
- Attended your next oncology conference with a new mind-set, to analyze what worked and what didn't work in the presentations, to visualize yourself giving a presentation based on the core ideas of

your book, to examine the relevant self-help titles in the conference bookstore, and to network a little with conference organizers.

- Jotted down notes for the book whenever a thought struck you.
- Gathered up some of the popular books on surviving cancer that you own and put them all in one bookcase.
- Circled a long weekend on your calendar when you'd begin your book in earnest.

> *And this is the way a novel gets written: in ignorance, fear, sorrow, madness, and a kind of psychotic happiness as an incubator for the wonders being born.*
> — JACK KEROUAC

- Said to yourself first thing each morning, "I get to start the book in twenty-three days. I'm really looking forward to it!" "I get to start the book in twenty-two days. I'm really looking forward it!" And so on.

Each of the steps that supports incubating a creative project is in itself simple, as simple as wondering to yourself "What advice would I like to offer cancer patients?" But these simple steps are deep steps, because they allow for the miracle of birth.

EXERCISE **39** • *Incubate a New Project*

Purchase a bag of large plastic Easter eggs and have ready twelve small slips of paper.

Put yourself in mind of a future creative project and give it a name, something simple like "that dessert cookbook" or "a new theory about the ego." Write the name on each slip of paper, fold up the slips, and put one in each of a dozen eggs.

Hide the eggs where you'll run into them regularly—one in the freezer, one in the laundry basket, one in the glove compartment, and so forth. When you encounter one of your eggs, open it up and read the message inside. Then say "Yes." Nod. Think about your dessert cookbook for a few seconds. If you want to pay it more attention than that, by all means do so. You could even stop what you were doing and launch right into some creative work.

Maybe you don't have a creative project in mind right now. Maybe you have one in mind but it's so far out of conscious awareness that it can't be named or accessed. In that case, put a question mark in each of the eggs. When you come upon one of your eggs, open it, unfold the slip of paper, and wonder to yourself what the question mark signifies. What's brewing? What life is growing?

WEEK 20

40. Expand with the Universe

During this month of exploring the concept of depth, I've made considerable use of the linguistic fact that the word "deep" means both "profound" and "at a great distance beneath a surface." But there are other important ways to think about "deep" in addition to "going down." "Deep" is also:

- the opposite of thoughtless
- the opposite of rote
- the opposite of incomplete
- the opposite of artificial
- the opposite of conventional
- the opposite of scattered
- the opposite of impersonal

- the opposite of narrow

Consider the last. Let's assume that you're a businessperson with a particular product or service to sell. You could have an intimate (and deep) understanding of the current markets for your particular product or service, but

> *Each conquest of distance reveals greater distance.*
> — MARTIN MARTY

if you haven't encouraged yourself to think about the relationship of your industry to other industries or to envision the future of your product or service, you might have a narrow (and not deep) understanding of the complete universe in which your business operated. If you could explain to me why the company for which you work instituted its particular hiring practices, emergency readiness plan, or marketing strategies, but not whether your industry was on the verge of such radical change that there'd be no place left in it for you, it'd be fair to say that you had a deep understanding of your business in one sense but not in another.

One of my students turned in an essay on the hiring practices in the biology lab where she worked. On her paper I commented, "You are covering how and why *you* hire this or that person beautifully, but you're not speaking to hiring in general or how hiring practices might be the same or different in other industries." She came up to me after class and said ironically, "I guess I just have bad breadth." Most of us have "bad breadth." Sometimes this is called "thinking in the box" or "a failure to make remote associations." We focus deeply but narrowly on the thing right in front of us, for instance on the details of our job, and have little mind space left over for broader, expansive thinking.

An everyday creative person grows accustomed to using "breadth" and "depth" interchangeably. She wants her novel to do justice to her characters, whom she hopes are unique and individual, but she also wants her novel to resonate in some unfathomable way with meanings from all over, from every corner of the galaxy. She wants her literary barrio to smell and feel like the barrio she knew growing up, but she also wants it to connect to barrios everywhere, to neighborhoods where they wear yarmulkes or speak Chinese. She wants to go deep as in down and deep as in wide.

> *Those who are willing to be vulnerable move among mysteries.*
> — THEODORE ROETHKE

Take some time to think about the different senses of the phrase "going deep." No phrase comes closer to capturing the essence of creativity.

EXERCISE **40** • *Expand with the Universe*

Expand your horizons. First, get your current creative project in mind. Imagine that you're on the moon and that your creative project is back here on earth. You can see your novel or sculpture perfectly clearly from where you sit on your moon perch, your manuscript or statue standing out like the Great Wall of China. In addition, you get to see the world that surrounds and affects your creative project, the one in which it is embedded and to which it must relate.

Study your creative project in this large context. Would it work better if it were informed by something over that way, from sub-Saharan Africa? Would it be richer if it took into account the global economy or the globalization of information? Can you spot the additional voices that need to be added to your documentary or your historical novel? Can you see how you've artificially separated your ideas about instincts in your current article from your ideas about innate violence in your last article? Does your Great Wall need to moved from China to Brazil?

Sit for a while on the moon, studying your creative project from a distance, so that you can see the trees *and* the forest. You may notice something vital about its details or even about its central concept.

PART 6

Use Yourself

Weeks 21-24

41. Hire Yourself as a Consultant

Part of you understands that you are your own best resource when it comes to creating. No one but you can figure out what will make your painting or your poem come alive. But, like most people, you may have to fight through psychological barriers before you see yourself as smart enough, experienced enough, and worthy enough to hire as your own consultant. We will pay an expert hundreds of dollars an hour for legal, financial, or psychotherapeutic advice, but we're unwilling to pay ourselves the courtesy of trusting that our own instincts and knowledge can guide us to the successful completion of our creative projects. Too often we doubt that we have the right information, ideas, and skills—in short, the right stuff—and dismiss our own expertise.

> *Each wood has its own purpose. I make masks out of alder, red cedar is for the large totem poles, and birch is good for rattles; it is harder and gives a better sound.*
>
> — DEMPSEY BOB

When I give my adult students an assignment—say, to write about the subject of divorce, parenting, or supervision at work—their first tendency is to consult books and see what "experts" have said on the matter. If I were interested in an academic, research-oriented essay this might be an appropriate way for them to tackle the assignment, but I've already explained to them that I'm interested in an essay based on their personal experience. I want to know what *they have* managed to learn from their experience with divorce, parenting, or supervision.

They can glance at books to refresh their memory about certain terms, but no book can tell them what they've learned from their own experiences. They could hire the most expensive divorce attorney as a consultant, but that consultant still couldn't get into their shoes. They have only one consultant to hire: themselves. And they do it. Over the course of ten weeks they write five essays full of their own insights and conclusions.

This is a transformative time. These students had no idea they could manage such a thing. The firefighters in my class knew they could run into burning buildings; the detectives knew they could solve homicides. But neither knew that they had learned anything about the grief process from their divorce or anything about communication skills from their marriage until they consulted with themselves during the essay-writing process.

> *I have moved from planes to lines. This happened one day when I tried to draw a waterfall: the line was the only thing that had speed enough.*
> — ARTHUR DOVE

For each of them a moment arrives, usually in the third or fourth week, when they surrender to the idea that it is appropriate to use themselves as their primary resource. From then on they become creative.

One student, in explaining why the process of turning to herself for advice felt so difficult, said "I think we've all become 'I aversive.'" This is an accurate observation. Our job now is to recondition ourselves and accept that we are the expert.

EXERCISE **41A** • *Write a Personal Article*

Write an article about something you've experienced. Pick an important event, then sit down with yourself and say, "Okay, self. Advise me how to write this."

Say it's a bulimic episode. Write down everything leading up to the binge: the gnawing hunger, the desperation, the shopping for Oreos and Fritos, the gorging, the puking, how bad that felt, and also how good. When you get stuck, turn to yourself and say, "Mary, what was going on that night? Am I right in thinking that it had something to do with Dad? And Mom, too?" Mary will know. Maybe she'll answer you right away. Maybe she'll have to sleep on it. But she'll get you the answer.

Hire yourself as a consultant. You know your stuff and the price is right.

EXERCISE **41B** • *Start a Savings Account*

Probably there's something special you'd like to treat yourself to, like a vacation in Provence or a new computer. Open up a savings account expressly for the purpose of paying for this special treat.

How much are you worth an hour? Plenty! But since you'll be paying yourself in this exercise, you'll have to be reasonable. Pick a piece of creative work you've been meaning to do, one that you've been putting off. Let's say it's outlining a new nonfiction book. Have the following conversation with yourself: "I need your help outlining my new book. I'll pay you thirty dollars an hour for six hours worth of work today. Deal?" Then take yourself to a cafe or to your study and work for six hours. Use yourself. Ask yourself questions and answer them. Then, the first chance you get, deposit $180 in your special savings account.

42. Open a Vein

Very soon after the birth of our first child, my wife and I decided that we wanted a second child. We (that is, she) got pregnant quickly, two or three months after Natalya's birth—and in retrospect, probably too quickly. It might have been wiser to let a few more eggs slip by. But we didn't and, for whatever reason, we produced an unhealthy fetus.

There is nothing quite like going in for a routine sonar imaging appointment and seeing a look of distress appear on the faces of the technicians. It turned out that the fetus had Down's syndrome—and if that had been the only problem, I'm not sure what we would have done. Maybe we would have gone forward. But the fetus was also severely hydrocephalic— she had water on the brain—and the odds were great that she wouldn't survive to term and that the pregnancy would be toxic to my wife—even lethal.

We had the abortion. As sometimes happens when the stress in my life is high, I got sick; and so a friend of my wife's had to take her to the hospital for the procedure. To recuperate, we packed up our infant daughter, got on a plane, and went to Hawaii. As a result, Natalya took her first steps in a sushi bar in Honolulu. Our pictures of that time show two people on the mend. Not too much later we had a second child, a daughter, Kira, whom we wouldn't have had if that fetus had lived. But all that good luck doesn't change the fact that we experienced something dreadful.

I possess the information about that pregnancy intellectually, viscerally, in terms of sights and sounds, as thoughts and feelings, in every way that a thing like that can be known to a man. I know how a fever can rise up suddenly and strike down a healthy person. I know how two people can cry without shedding any tears. I can use all of this; I am using it here. I must use it, if I am to write truthfully. If we want to create things that live, we need to access our feelings as well as our thoughts and be willing to pour our blood into our creative efforts. Blood has its place in the creative process—shed right into the work.

> *If we would really feel, the pain would be so great that we would stop all the suffering.*
> — JULIAN BECK

Whatever pain and suffering you've experienced in your life has been a blessing at least in this one regard: you now know some true things that you couldn't have learned any other way. When you sculpt, you can let in anguish if anguish is called for. When you write, you can pierce your reader's heart. You can design homes for human beings and let real life into your social science. You would not have asked to experience the pain you did, but now you can make some use of it.

But what if you've decided, consciously or not, to keep your deep feelings out of your creative efforts? Well, then, change your mind! If you won't shed your blood right into your art, I fear for your process and your products. You may say, "I'm a physicist and none of this has any meaning for me." I would strongly disagree. A desire to be all brain and no feelings has its ramifications, not only in your personal life but also in your creative life. Your unacknowledged and unaccessed pain—about a relationship failure, about your life's work not winning or warranting the Nobel prize, about the envy you feel toward a colleague, about anything that's hurt you—

is likely to be an anchor keeping your thoughts from soaring. If you acknowledge your pain and allow yourself a new freedom to feel, you will liberate your best thinking.

As an artist, you reach for the pen that's full of blood.

— PAUL MONETTE

If you're a scientist, say to yourself, "No more dry articles! I'm going to leave traces of my blood!" If you're a poet with a penchant for artifice, say "No more academic poetry! I'll write the equivalent of bloodstains!" If you're a composer with an intellectual bent, say, "No more brilliance! I want to draw tears from my audience!" Make a commitment to feel and not just think.

EXERCISE **42** • *Open a Vein*

Over the next three days, write a detailed personal essay in which you recount a painful episode you lived through. Do this exercise even if your creative discipline is subatomic physics or software applications.

Then go a step farther. Show your essay to another person. Acknowledge that you've bled in the past; and bleed even as you write your essay, for the sake of your creativity and your humanity.

WEEK 22

43. Get Ravenous

In Kafka's famous short story, his character the Hunger Artist became a world-renowned circus attraction because he could fast so well. Day after day he sat in front of burgeoning crowds, not eating. But he refused to take credit for his unusual talent. He simply shrugged and explained that he fasted because food bored him. Nothing had ever awakened his taste buds. Food tasted to him like cardboard, like dirt. Not only would he have broken his fast if something had tasted good, he'd even have gorged himself. But nothing did. So, passive and indifferent, he sat and starved himself.

> *Acting was like hunger in the pit of my stomach, and if I didn't cater to it, it got worse.*
> — ANDY GARCIA

We nod at the Hunger Artist's explanation of his fasting, because it has a ring of truth to it. But what lies beneath his words? Has he injured his taste buds? Is he suffering from some odd medical affliction that prevents him from enjoying food's savoriness and saltiness? Was it his bad luck to encounter too many canned peas and carrots in his youth? How can food be *that* boring? Truthfully, he hasn't explained himself at all.

People need food to live. It seems logical that we would eat even if the food in front of us didn't tantalize us. Wouldn't our instincts override matters of taste? But maybe they wouldn't. For aren't millions of us "not eating" in our own ways: not creating, not living with gusto, not bringing love and passion to our daily life? Like the Hunger Artist, people in this situation are deeply bored and apathetic: their instinct to enjoy life is not powerful enough to counteract their feelings of meaninglessness.

Meaninglessness is the Hunger Artist's real problem and the problem of millions of our contemporaries. When the Hunger Artist says that food has never interested him, he is saying an existential mouthful. Psychologically defeated, pessimistic, and doubting that life is worth living, many people feel as disconnected from life as the Hunger Artist is disconnected from food. They know in a corner of consciousness that they're starving for meaning yet they feel oddly indifferent, like a person in the last stages of death by freezing. If someone says, "Why not try your hand at writing a novel?" they yawn and reply, "No, no thanks. I think not. No novel writing for me. I'm fine. Maybe someday. Who knows? But not today, no, thank you." What they're really saying is, "I'm in despair. Leave me alone."

> *Painting slows down a complex world for me. It allows time for the study of a leaf or a rock. It satisfies a hunger in me.*
> — LYNN SCHWARTZ

The Hunger Artist needs a reason to eat, not the right food. The same is true for many of us. We don't need the right computer; we need a reason to write. We don't need a special dance space; we need a reason to dance. In order to create, you need reasons to create; then your natural appetites, your lust for life, your desire for sweets and barbecue and big creative projects will return.

Once life feels meaningful, your appetite returns of its own accord. But if your life doesn't feel meaningful, you can still try to birth new meaning by telling yourself that you're ravenous. If the Hunger Artist had had a shred of hope left, he might have been able to will himself to exclaim, "Damn, that salami looks good! I'll give it a try!" Having tasted it—having tasted life again—he might have begun to recover. Acting *as if* you're ravenous is one cure for existential malaise.

EXERCISE **43** • *Get Ravenous*

Today, really make your mouth water.

Start by picking an object of desire: a new poem you want to write, a new fabric you want to design, a new song you want to compose. Now, lick your lips right up in the corners. Picture that delicious poem as if it were the best dish ever cooked, the smell of it wafting your way, its perfume so powerful that your knees begin to buckle. Don't you want it? Aren't you aching for it? Aren't you salivating?

Spend as much of the next three days as you can feeling like a person rescued at sea. You've almost died of exposure, but now you've been picked up by a cruise ship. You can have massages with exotic oils. You can have rich soups redolent of thyme, mushrooms, and red wine. You can have whatever you want, around the clock.

In this context, write your new poem or song. Write it over an imaginary brunch of smoked salmon, capers, and onions. Revise it at a make-believe high tea of scones, blackberry jam, and clotted cream. In your mind, get dressed for dinner and bring your poem or song and your still-ravenous feelings to a meal that begins with champagne and ends with something flaming. Feel savage in your hunger. Don't forget the midnight buffet! Create ravenously and go to sleep sated.

WEEK 22

44. Undepress

When you're hurting, it's hard—often even impossible—to create. Suffering from emotional problems, many accomplished creators have seen their output diminish to nothing and their lives end in ruin because of psychological pain. For the few years that Jackson Pollock refrained from drinking alcohol and achieved some emotional balance, he produced some of the finest paintings of the century. When he fell off the wagon and succumbed to his inner distress, he managed only a few more paintings—mostly in black—and was dead in six years. Our inner pain does not benefit us, any myths of that sort notwithstanding. Psychological problems like severe depression, acute anxiety, and addictions are curses, not blessings.

Yesterday, happiness came in suddenly, as it used to, and remained for a moment in the great, dark, silent drawing room.

— JULIEN GREEN

Everyday creative people are highly likely to suffer from emotional problems like depression. When they do, they are the first—and really the only—line of defense against the crushing power of emotional distress. Mental institutions do not make people well. Psychiatrists are not mental health magicians. NA and AA do not cure addictions. Medications can be part of the answer but are never the whole answer. If you're experiencing psychological pain, you will have to provide your own answers and your own curatives.

This may strike you as a heretical view. Isn't clinical depression an illness requiring medical treatment? Maybe. But even if it is, who is in charge of taking the prescribed medication? You are. Who has to make use of whatever psychotherapy can offer? You do. Who has to inaugurate the changes that will help you heal and recover? You.

In order to achieve mental health, we have to make use of our own gifts, our own wisdom, our own love of life, and our own powers of persuasion. How hard this can be! The creative personality is a rich nutrient soil in which an affliction like depression naturally grows. The qualities an everyday creative person manifests, like empathy, compassion, and thought-fulness, produce a person who feels sorrow, knows failure, experiences alienation, and grows tired of the ordinary. She can become depressed easily and often.

Then if she writes books that she cannot sell, if she loves to dance but her body type is not wanted in the marketplace, if she needs to paint but hates the canvases she produces, or if she emerges from childhood with an anxious personality that interferes with her ability to perform powerfully at auditions, that depresses her further. I once made a list of the things that depress creative people and that list, which included everything from problems concentrating to dispiriting day jobs, ran to seven single-spaced pages.

If you be not ill,
be not ill-like.
— SCOTTISH PROVERB

Who do we know who has been depressed? Emily Dickinson. Charles Dickens. William Faulkner. William Blake. Leo Tolstoy. Mark Twain. Virginia Woolf. Berlioz, Beethoven, Handel, Mahler, Rossini and Tchaikovsky. Gauguin, van Gogh, Michelangelo, O'Keeffe, and Pollock. Even people you have never heard of in your life. One out of every one artist. Maybe you. Certainly me.

EXERCISE 44 • *Create a Depression*
Treatment Plan

The following are steps you can take to deal with a depression or other emotional problem. Take time now to think through these steps and flesh out the plan with your own observations. Then, when a psychological injury occurs, put the plan into action as quickly as possible.

1. Talk. Air your feelings to another person, to your cat, to yourself when you're alone. It's liberating to speak your truth, pain and all, out loud.
2. Make an effort to find reasons to be hopeful. Envision a future success, remind yourself that you can still be a loving presence in the world, suggest to yourself that life is mysterious enough that answers to your problems may become available.
3. Challenge your negative thinking. Say to yourself, "I appear to be very down on myself and on my life, but I am still going to talk to myself in a loving and encouraging way."
4. Focus on any positive changes you've been implementing in your life, like sobriety or intimate relating. Keep working on them.
5. Look for any feelings—sadness, anger, bitterness, envy, grief, loneliness—that may be generating your emotional pain.
6. Ask for help—from friends, relatives, counselors, even from strangers on a telephone hot line.

Your emotional health is in your hands. Use the best of you to help the rest of you.

45. Kill Maybe

Over the years I've come to realize the power of the three little words "yes," "no," and "maybe." It has turned out to be much more effective to frame my therapeutic work in terms of the ideas embedded in these three words than to indulge in fancy psychological theories or resort to clever psychotherapeutic technique.

What do I mean by this? Well, if I help a client break free of maybe and say yes and no in new ways, startling growth and healing can occur. After two phone consultations, one famous singer-songwriter on the verge of refusing to record his latest album could switch his mind from "Maybe I need more time to prepare" to "Yes, I can record right now." By making that switch he found the courage and the will to enter the studio. One well-known guitarist I worked with was able to move from the maybe of playing music that she didn't love to the yes of forming her own band. By moving from maybe to yes, an actor could begin her performance piece and a painter could try his hand at larger, more ambitious paintings. Both in our personal and our creative lives, good things happen when we learn to champion yes.

> *I get up at six in the morning. I wear cotton clothes so that I can sleep in them or I can work in them—I don't want to waste time. Sometimes I work two or three days without sleeping and without paying attention to food.*
>
> — LOUISE NEVELSON

Why then do we usually say maybe, rather than yes? Mainly because we learn through hard experience that even when we manage to say yes, we get very mixed results. Only sometimes do we feel good about our accomplishments. Often we seem to make matters worse. It's bad not to be painting if painting is our dream, but how much better is it to stand in front of a blank canvas feeling empty and stupid, not knowing how to proceed? Worse than staying in maybe and not painting. If and when we do begin to paint, we're likely to make a mess. How good does that feel? Not very good at all. Maybe we survive that blow and manage to say yes a second time with a new canvas. What happens then? We make a second mess. Now we feel dreadful! Disappointed with ourselves, we sink back into maybe, convinced that maybe, as painful as it feels, is better than the fruitless yesses we just experienced.

Since we often get these very mixed results from saying yes, we begin to wonder if doing so is worth the effort. Why bother? If doing all the work required to write a good short story only nets us a single one we like out of a dozen attempts, why bother? If blowing

> *Teach yourself to work in uncertainty.*
> — BERNARD MALAMUD

the whistle on a shady practice at work only brings us a reprimand, why bother? If having a talk with our son only leads to a fight, why not let things slide? Why not just stay in maybe, which may not get us what we want but at least avoids some anguish?

We know why. Each of us knows why we shouldn't hang out in maybe. But still we get trapped there. Here's how the maybe trap sounds when we're in its clutches:

1. There's a novel you're hoping to start. You say to yourself, "Maybe I'll get to it next week."
2. You want to make a work space so that you can paint, but that would mean asking your husband to clean out his junk from the spare room. You say, "Maybe I'll talk to him in the spring, when he's less busy."

These maybes are the equivalent of lies. When you're caught in the maybe trap you're living the equivalent of a lie. Here's the truth behind each of these maybes.

1. I'm unwilling to begin my novel.
2. I'm scared to ask for what I need, and I'm especially scared to ask my husband.

Here's what yes sounds like.

1. I'm starting my novel right now.
2. I'm talking to John this evening.

Yes may lead to difficulties, but maybe leads nowhere. Kill it.

EXERCISE 45 • *Kill Maybe and Champion Yes*

L isten to yourself this week. When you say something that sounds exactly or suspiciously like maybe, stop yourself. If, for example, you hear yourself say, "Maybe I'll practice the flute tomorrow," exclaim, "Die, maybe!" Champion yes instead. Say, "Yes, I will practice the flute today!" If you hear yourself say, "I wonder if there's enough time to work on my story?" exclaim, "Die, maybe!" Proceed with, "Yes, of course there's enough time!" Since every yes of this sort is a call to action, your job is also to do the work required to turn your new yes into a reality.

WEEK 23

46. Build a Model Creator

I magine that you could build a human being from scratch and wanted to make sure that she'd turn out to be everyday creative. What traits would you give her? According to the creativity literature and from my own observations working with creative clients, I think that you'd want to incorporate the following seventy-five traits for a start.

1. Access to emotions
2. Alert to gaps in knowledge
3. Ambitiousness
4. Anxiety tolerance
5. Asks "Why?" questions
6. Assertiveness
7. Breadth of knowledge
8. Compassion
9. Concentration
10. Confidence
11. Convergent thinking abilities
12. Copes with novelty
13. Courage
14. Creativity
15. Creativity in a domain
16. Curiosity
17. Decision-making capabilities
18. Depth of knowledge
19. Discipline
20. Divergent thinking abilities
21. Empathy
22. Energy
23. Evaluative abilities
24. Existential outlook
25. Flexibility
26. Honesty
27. Humanitarianism
28. Imagination
29. Ingenuity
30. Intellectual honesty
31. Intellectual playfulness
32. Intelligence
33. Interest in challenges
34. Interest in problems
35. Interest in solutions
36. Intrinsically motivated
37. Introspective stance
38. Intuition
39. Love of beauty
40. Love of complexity
41. Love of doubt
42. Love of freedom
43. Love of goodness
44. Love of language
45. Love of logic
46. Love of mystery
47. Love of simplicity
48. Metaphoric thinking abilities
49. Moral outlook
50. Nonconformity
51. Openness to experience
52. Optimism
53. Originality
54. Passion
55. Patience
56. Persistence
57. Playfulness
58. Pleasure capabilities
59. Questions norms/assumptions
60. Reality-testing abilities
61. Resiliency
62. Risk-taking orientation
63. Self-centeredness
64. Self-direction
65. Self-trust
66. Sense of humor
67. Sensitivity
68. Seriousness
69. Skepticism
70. Spiritual outlook
71. Thoughtfulness
72. Tolerance
73. Tolerance for ambiguity
74. Unconcern with social approval
75. Uses knowledge base

Of course you'd have a tricky time getting these qualities put together in just the right proportions.

> *No words can describe the immense tenderness of Diego for the things which had beauty. He tried to do what he considered just in life: to work and create.*
>
> — FRIDA KAHLO, ON HER HUSBAND, DIEGO RIVERA

You'd want to make sure that your creative person's skepticism didn't slide into nihilism, that her love of goodness didn't make her a patsy, that her energy didn't cross a line into mania. You'd want her to have a healthy self-centeredness and not an unhealthy narcissism; you'd hope that her love of complexity didn't cause her to choose only insoluble problems to tackle; you'd pray that her love of freedom didn't make her unemployable, and so on. You can see what a hard job it would be to effectively combine all of these traits, some of which contradict one another, into the same person.

But this is exactly what each of us must do. These are the traits that an everyday creative person hopes to manifest, in just the right proportions and in just the right combination. As a creative person, you may possess some of these traits in large measure. You may be highly intelligent or stubbornly self-directing. In other areas you may be weaker. Maybe you aren't optimistic or assertive enough, or maybe you care too much about social approval. But with this list in hand, you can identify any such lacks and decide to work on them one trait at a time.

EXERCISE 46 • *Take a Multi-Vitamin*

Isolating one of the seventy-five traits and working on it can be a rewarding experience. You can decide to become a better risk-taker, for example, focusing just on that trait and inventing exercises and tasks that help you take new risks. On Day One you could decide to tackle a project whose bigness frightens you. On Day Two you could make the risky-feeling decision to commit to completing the project come hell or high water. On Day Three you could risk ridicule, embarrassment, indifference, or that look that says, "You think you have *that* in you?" by telling your friends, "I've decided to write a novel about the history of the universe."

> *In terms of both talent and behavior, Degas is a rare example of what an artist should be.*
> — PAUL GAUGUIN

Tackling all seventy-five traits at once is a mind-boggling idea, but working this way one trait at a time is eminently doable. Put up this list of personality traits somewhere where you can access it easily, say on the door of your refrigerator. As part of your morning ritual, go to the list and read it over. Take it in, but don't worry about doing anything. Reading it in a thoughtful way each morning is the equivalent of taking a one-a-day creativity multi-vitamin.

WEEK 24

47. Look Where You Slipped

We make lots of mistakes in life, including some very painful ones. We often slip and fall. If we aren't careful, these slips thoroughly dispirit us and block us. Therefore, as an everyday creative person, you will need to do three things: pick yourself up when you slip, affirm that you're continuing to create, and figure out how that banana peel got there in the first place. The more you understand why you slipped, the better chance you have to prevent some future pratfalls.

Let me tell you about one of my better mistakes.

My first novel, a picaresque about GIs in Korea, somehow found its way to a well-known literary agent. A friend of mine to whom I'd sent the novel sent it to his friend who in turn sent it to the agent, so when I received her letter it came as a complete surprise. Here is that letter, dated March 15, 1978.

> *Do not look where you fell, but where you slipped.*
>
> — AFRICAN PROVERB

Dear Eric,

Your manuscript was recently referred to our office. We like it very much, and feel we have a good possibility of getting it published as a love story if you can find the time to revise it a bit. We suggest that it be cut to about 250 pages, with a strong focus on the relationship between Jon and Annie. The writing style is exceptionally fine, and the characters are interesting. We've clipped some readers' comments onto various sections and lifted out the pages we suggest you cut.

The passages about Jon's army life that don't relate directly to Jon and Annie are, in my opinion, somewhat distracting. I suggest you try to define Jon's outlook on love and women more clearly (why does he react to Annie as a woman of danger? As far as I can see from any actual action she takes, she is just young and confused, not self-destructive or wild). You might consider working in a good kidnap plot—let Ivan or Annie's father whisk her away, then let Jon be the hero and save the day.

I hope you'll find time to devote to this end and, if you do, I feel it will be well worth your while.

Sincerely, Ms. Agent

What was my reaction to this letter? I told her to go to hell. Why? For many bad reasons. I didn't want anyone telling me anything. I didn't want to sully my novel with plot. I didn't want to have to re-work it and, worse, retype it. I wanted someone to say, "This is great as is and ready to be published." It never occurred to me that this was a positive and even flattering letter, that the amount of time the agent and her associate had spent on it was far more than agents typically spend on manuscripts, and that I should be thankful, feel myself lucky, and make the suggested changes. None of that crossed my mind. I answered in a huff that no novel of mine would ever sport a gratuitous kidnapping.

I seldom try to probe the mystery of my sloth. Because of it, I have squandered a gigantic fortune of work hours. Now, with a life expectancy of 8.5 years, it seems likely that I'll go on squandering till the very end.

— CHRISTOPHER ISHERWOOD

Of course the novel was never published.

This happened a long time ago. But I haven't stopped slipping. In 1996, I sold a book based on a proposal that I didn't believe in. What might I have done differently? Not shopped that proposal around. As I began writing the book, I could feel myself taking shortcuts. If a chapter cried out for substantiation, I used a make-believe example instead of something from published case studies. What might I have done differently? I could have had a little chat with myself. "Eric, don't do this. It won't work. You'll be sorry." But I didn't. Of course, that book turned out to be unpublishable.

I could go on. I didn't slip in just those two places but in many. But I am trying to figure out why, because I really do want to know. Won't you do the same? Won't you use your critical thinking skills and your other estimable resources, including your brave heart, in the service of examining the big mistakes you've made, the ones that feel like self-sabotage? I hope you will.

EXERCISE 47 • *Look Where You Slipped*

This may be painful to do. But I want you to recall a creative project that turned into a nasty spill. The bigger the spill, the more benefit you'll get from this exercise.

Pick a whopper, one where you really fell hard. Draw up a list of all the reasons for that spill, as many reasons as you can think of, not to allocate blame or to second-guess yourself but to understand what happened. After each reason, name one thing you might have done differently or would do differently now.

That fall is in the past, but your learning continues.

WEEK 24

48. Be Yourself Entirely

Carl Jung had the idea that we are born whole and then lose pieces of ourselves in the crucible of childhood. We lose our natural extroversion and become more and more introverted, or vice versa. We lose our ability to feel and put more and more stock in thinking, or vice versa. We become static and one-dimensional. The main task of midlife, Jung thought, was to weather the crisis that arises from this experience of loss and become a whole, integrated person again.

There is no better place to do this integrative work than as you create. You can use the resources you currently have to recover the parts of you that may have gotten lost. If you are too intellectual, you can choose an emotional subject to write about and bring tears to your own eyes. If you are too easily distracted, you can learn from your pottery practice how to center a vase and center yourself in the process. If you feel you are too "normal," you can act so weird as you create your performance piece that, if someone saw you, he'd have no choice but to report you.

> *It requires great daring to dare to be oneself.*
> — EUGÈNE DELACROIX

When you finally become yourself, you reap many benefits. You have more of you to use for your future creative efforts and for all of life's challenges— more energy, more passion, more flexibility, more discipline, more imagination. You become multifaceted, not one-dimensional, and whole, not fractured. When you manage this reintegration, you become the very embodiment of an everyday creative person.

EXERCISE **48A** • *Identify the Authentic You*

Take a few hours today and try to answer the following questions.

1. What parts of your authentic self have you lost during the course of living your life? For example, are you less spontaneous, playful, thoughtful, compassionate, or daring than you were as a child? Can you identify those parts of your personality that have gotten submerged over time?
2. What have been the consequences of these losses? How are you different from the way you would have been if you'd remained whole and integrated?

3. Are there any creative projects you might want to embark on specifically for the purpose of reconnecting with a lost part of your personality?

4. Can you paint a word picture of what an integrated, authentic you would look like? How would you spend your days? What creative work would you do?

EXERCISE **48B** • *Wear Your Own Clothes*

Off with your public clothing! Let's dress the new authentic you.

What would an integrated you wear? A T-shirt and shorts? A sari? An Armani suit? Nothing at all? For me, purple sweat pants and a red sweatshirt work well. What works for you? Put those clothes on. (If you don't own them, you'll have to purchase them first.)

Now, go someplace. You—you entirely—decide where. Maybe it's to the local peach orchard to pick peaches. Maybe it's to the llama farm for some llama conversation. Or maybe it's into the tub with a book on Gothic arches.

At the llama farm, be you. Sit in the dirt. Don't be embarrassed. Talk to the llamas. Run with the llama farmer's dog. At the peach orchard, bite into a peach with your authentic bite, the full bite of your birthright. In the tub, read for hours, until you're as wrinkled as a prune. When you've finished this exercise, go straight to your creative work, holding in mind the idea that you have your entire personality at your disposal.

EXERCISE **48C** • *Take Stock*

For the past month you've investigated the idea of using yourself. For six months you've been growing into an everyday creative person. This is a good time to take stock of your progress so far. Write down your answers to the following questions.

> *We did not change as we grew older; we just became more clearly ourselves.*
>
> — LYNN HALL

- Have you launched into a large creative project, one worth exhausting yourself on? If not, can you identify why?
- Have you been doing the exercises or just reading along?
- Have you constructed a schedule for your creative work and are you keeping to it? Do you set goals at the beginning of each week? Do you have a daily routine that supports your creative efforts?

PART 7

Connect

Weeks 25-28

49. Go Out

It is fine to sit in your study and create. But it is equally fine, and sometimes better, to do your creating away from home while surrounded by your fellow creatures. We get some of our best ideas and often feel emotionally our best when sitting on a bench in the town square with our writing pad open, at a table on the terrace of our favorite cafe with our sketchbook ready, or by the public pool listening to the laughter of children with our flute handy.

The world is an everyday creative person's second home. It is free, and it is yours. You can experience a subway hurtling through Manhattan, a postmodern Tex-Mex cafe, a path by the river, or Papa Joe's pizzeria each as an excellent second home, good for the heart and good for the mind, if you bring your notebook with you—and a willingness to open it. But that willingness is crucial.

Many people are embarrassed to create in public. It feels unseemly to them, like kissing in plain view. Pulling out a writing pad in public heightens their self-consciousness and makes them feel foolish. But really—who is justified in pulling out her pad and writing right in the middle of a restaurant? You are. Who is not showing off in some narcissistic way but simply creating when an idea hits her and she sits down on the sidewalk to record it? You are. Who is not ridiculous or phony or eccentric or arrogant if she excuses herself and stops in mid-conversation to capture a phrase that she's been stalking for a week? You. You have that right and that responsibility.

An important part of an everyday creative

person's education is learning to create in public. You will learn that you are sufficiently insulated in the world, even as you are out and about in it. No one will pay you any mind. No one will hold it against you if you write poetry on the bus. No one will care if you do a little physics while you wait in line. And if someone does, forgive him. He must belong to a religion where creativity is unimportant.

Like a bird who, when his cage is opened, stays on his perch, dazzled by freedom, the postponed traveler does not see that his cage, with its bars of anxiety, is open.

— ANDRÉ MAUROIS

EXERCISE **49A** • *Go Out*

Go out today with the intention to create. Take a pad, several pens, an apple, your current idea, and anything else you need to spend three or four hours in the world.

Go somewhere you'd never think of going to write, draw, or think. Go to a bank, settle into one of their plush chairs, and create. Go to a parking lot rather than a bookstore, stand next to a pickup truck, and create. When someone looks at you, say to yourself, "Hello, fellow creature!" and not, "Oh, I'd better move on." Own the world. When a thought strikes, jot it down. Stop whenever and wherever you like.

Make a spectacle of yourself. The world needs more spectacular sights. People need to see the creative process in action. When you create in the world, you serve yourself but you also remind others what creating looks like and that they too could be participating. In this way, you proselytize for the religion of creativity and make new converts.

Make several trips into the world this week. Each time you go out, remind yourself that you are an everyday creative person dedicated to creating in even the most unlikely places. Find a few of those unlikely places and do some excellent work.

EXERCISE **49B** • *Live the Coffee House Life*

Let one of your forays into the world be to a neighborhood coffee house.

Most communities have a local coffee house or two, a Barnes and Noble with a cafe, or a Starbucks. But if your community doesn't, come as close as you can to the coffee house experience. Maybe the art department at the local junior college has a lounge. Maybe there's a luncheonette on Main Street with a slightly arty atmosphere. My hunch is that you'll find something.

> *I have always felt more natural working out of doors.*
> — LOUIS SIEGRIEST

Say to yourself, "I'm part of the coffee house tradition. I can sit for hours, nurse a double espresso, enjoy the spectacle, and do some fine creating." Watch people. Then bury your head for a while and create. Notice how easy it is to enter the trance of working. Notice how pure silence engulfs you, even though the espresso machine is chattering and folks are conversing. This is one of your homes. Come back any time.

WEEK 25

50. Visit with Children

While staying in Budapest, my wife and I boarded a tram one summer morning. We had no idea where it was going, but we jumped aboard anyway. The tram left the city and slowly began climbing a mountain. At each stop up that mountain we saw children playing—the higher up, the older the children. Each group displayed banners of the sort that suburban parents in America make for their children's soccer teams.

We had happened upon a state-sponsored summer camp. But although state-sponsored, the end of the state was written in the attitude of these children. We might never have guessed the imminent fall of communist regimes in Eastern Europe from watching the evening news at home; however, those events could have been anticipated from watching these children. They looked altogether too joyous and independent-minded to stand for a lifetime of subjugation.

On the day I think I'll be free to write, her school is called off because of snow. But then my daughter and I will have a great talk, or she'll discover something that changes the world for the both of us.
— RITA DOVE

I learn a lot from children. Everything that I consider important is there for the knowing at a children's party, in the face of a newborn, or wherever children gather. It is my bias that our creative nature opens and our creativity grows if we visit with children. When I am sitting on the floor with a three-year-old, seriously turning a piece of foil from a package of gum into a three-legged giraffe, I feel myself in the right mood for anything—for touching another person's heart or for cracking a big idea wide open.

One visit with a child can supply us with enough magic creativity dust to last for a lifetime. But one visit would be too few! Visit with children, not as a critic, teacher, or caretaker but like you love them and want to make faces. Visit with them like you are three feet tall and sillier than any of them. Visit with them like you are a party about to happen. Visit with them . . . well, you get the idea. Visit with children like you're the child you ought to be more often.

EXERCISE 50 • *Visit with Children*

Spend a day where small children gather. The playground is a good spot. So is a grassy knoll by a zoo cafeteria or the benches by the fountain at an outdoor mall. Leave at home that part of you that is irritated or made nervous by children. Try to bring an open heart. Your only goals are to feel joyous, light, and sunny, to make some heart connections, to smile, to feel alive and appreciative. Just watch the children's antics and eavesdrop on their conversations. When you get home, sunburnt and a little sick from that second hot dog, take a nap if you need it. Then rise ready to create.

If you have children of your own, make some special time to enjoy them. Bring out the old pots and pans from the garage and join them in playing rock-and-roll music. Tie some old clothes together into a makeshift rope and have a tug-of-war. Get a CD of French children's songs and sing along. Feel like you're on vacation, and not on one of those miserable ones where everybody is grumpy and can't wait to get home. It really doesn't matter if your children are six, eleven, or thirty-nine. You can still visit with them in this playful, soulful, heartfelt way.

Or you might invite some of your friends' children over for an afternoon. Instead of doing any sketching yourself, give the children paper and crayons, a subject—an elephant parade, a day in the life of a screwdriver—and permission to go wild. Instead of writing your own poetry, invite their poems.

Instead of composing a song, teach them a round and join in. Let go of your worries and play along. Get the laughter going.

Tackling a gigantic subject with small children can be the most fun of all. As Plato himself might have, begin with a question like "What is justice?" The children will purse their lips, think a minute, and then tell you. They'll do a better job than a gaggle of pundits. I'd be surprised if the richness of their answers didn't provoke you to create as soon as your little guests departed.

I would rather see a wonderful little child than the Grand Canyon.
— ROBERT HENRI

But it can happen that visiting with children will make you feel despondent, not creative. Maybe you won't feel like working at all. Being with children can open old wounds or strike painful nerves. If that happens, try not to let the sadness prevent you from repeating the experience. It's just too important to keep up our contact with children, because they revive us and inspire our best stories. Try to spend a Sunday a month surrounded by children. In no time, your heart and your creations will show the difference.

WEEK 26

51. Buddy Up

Creativity is an individual activity. But finding other creative people with whom you interact and collaborate can help your solitary work. A good writer will be helped by a good editor. A good conductor will be helped by a good orchestra. A good director will be helped by a good screenwriter, good costumers, and good actors. Each of us is helped by a good art buddy—an everyday creative person like ourselves with whom we chat, exchange ideas, share our creative work, and give and get help.

Here's how the art buddy relationship works. When I have a new idea for a book, I call you up and tell you about it. You say, "That sounds interesting! I can't wait to see how you're going to handle that. It sounds like the natural follow-up to your last book. But I do have some concerns. Ready to hear about them?" Two months later, I send you the book proposal based on the idea. You read it, call me up, and say, "Well, the new proposal *is* interesting. But it's a little cold. It doesn't capture your warmth at all. And it's clever, but more clever than deep. There *is* one part that I love, though. Can I tell you about that part?"

> *Without him I would have given up.*
>
> — PIERRE AUGUSTE RENOIR, ON MONET

As you tell me these things, I feel myself smiling. I love it that I can get invaluable feedback of this sort from you before I approach agents and editors. I love it that you know my books and are able to relate this proposal to my other work. I love it that you have brains and a heart, just like me. I love it that two everyday creative people can enrich each other and worship the same religion. Does it bother me that you don't really like this proposal? No. First, you may be right, which means you're providing me with vital news. Second, I'll make up my own mind. Third, and most important, the benefits of having you treat my work carefully and respectfully far outweigh any pain I might feel.

For my part, when I hear about an editor who might be interested in what you write, you are the first to know. If you haven't sent out your latest proposal in a while, because the agents to whom you sent it didn't respond favorably or didn't respond at all, I call you up and wonder if you're ready to resubmit your proposal. If something about the marketing section of your proposal has been bothering me but I haven't been able to put my finger on the problem and then suddenly it hits me, I get right on the phone and tell you about my concern. In short, I think about you and your work, just as you think about me and my work.

Fashioning a successful art buddy relationship depends on where you are in your creative journey, whom you currently know, how much or how little contact you care to maintain with another person, what your personality allows for, whether or not you actually want your creative efforts seen by others, and similar important matters. If you are just starting out, you may find it painfully hard to hear criticism of your work, and the only art buddy you may want is one who never says anything unkind. Maybe you feel too secretive to show your work to another person, maybe you don't know anyone you can trust, maybe you have a secret desire to spare your ego rejection and don't want someone pushing you to contact gallery owners or publish your research findings.

Of great importance to me was meeting Bob Rauschenberg. He was a Southerner like me, near my own age, and seemed the first completely devoted artist I had known.

— JASPER JOHNS

But I hope you'll think about getting an art buddy. First, you need to think about whether you are good art buddy material yourself. Second, you need to find the right person and start to build a strong, useful relationship.

EXERCISE **51A** • *Become Art Buddy Material*

Make two charts. On the first chart, enter the pros of an art buddy relationship in one column and the cons in a second column, putting items like important feedback on the pro side and painful criticism on the con side. Study this chart and maybe even sleep with it. I hope you'll decide that the pros outweigh the cons.

On the second chart, enter your strengths and weaknesses as a potential art buddy, including items like empathy on the strength side and arrogance on the weakness side. Commit to any changes you would need to make to eliminate the problems you've identified.

EXERCISE **51B** • *Enter into an Art Buddy Relationship*

Ask someone to be your art buddy. Describe to him or her what that relationship entails, as best you understand it. Then begin the process. Show your new art buddy what you're working on. Ask to see what he or she is working on. Exchange ideas. Be mutually respectful. Grow together.

WEEK 26

52. Sing Together

Art gallery openings seem to me to be more often about gossip and the exercise of ego than about soulful celebration. Wrap parties at the end of the run of a play are more often about breaking off run-of-the-show love affairs than about sharing feelings of accomplishment. Three artists in a van, on the way to paint in the country, are more likely to be self-involved than to break into song. Only occasionally does anything soulful or celebratory occur when creative people gather.

> *Gauguin says that when sailors have to move a heavy load or raise an anchor, they all sing together to keep them up and give them vim. That's just what artists lack!*
>
> — VINCENT VAN GOGH

Why is this? First, because spirituality is more an interior matter than a communal affair in this religion of ours. Deep connections tend to be fostered between creative individuals and their work, rather than between one creative individual and another. There is real soulfulness in the editing room as a filmmaker connects with her images. There is even soulfulness in the hushed theater as the audience watches her film, because the audience is sharing in the filmmaker's spiritual adventure. But there is little soulfulness at the reception that follows the film's screening. There ego, appetite, and social anxiety take over.

Second, and more important, creative people find relating with one another difficult. Envy rears its head. Pride gets in the way. Rivalries erupt. Realistic painters square off against abstract painters. Poets who like feeling and poets who like thought ridicule one another. Horn players are snide about the strings, and string players reply that nothing good has ever come out of a tube. The shadow side of human nature grabs center stage and aggressiveness, self-consciousness, and defensiveness rule the day.

Third, participants at a gathering aren't consciously holding these events as celebrations of spirit. If they did, they might do a better job of moderating their egos and relating with their hearts. But no solemnity, ceremony, or ritual is usually attached to these moments. When people act on stage, they have the sense that the theater is a sacred space; but when they meet with their fellow actors for drinks, that soulfulness vanishes. When they join together to bring a big idea to fruition they feel connected and happy, but once the project is finished they quickly resume their everyday arm's-length attitude.

> *I have found in women's affection a peculiar understanding, a mothering quality. It is a fact that the people who have helped me most at difficult moments of my musical career, beginning with my own sister, Mary, have been members of my own sex.*
>
> — ETHEL SMYTH

If we could bring the same deep feelings to our relating that we bring to our best creative work, and if we could invest all our interactions with heart, welcome changes would occur. Creative people would begin to enjoy each other's company and benefit by becoming each other's mentor and audience member.

More soulful connecting among creators would be a good thing, because we need each other's help and we need each other's love. But to get there requires leadership. You may want to become just such a leader, a soulful master of ceremonies who organizes events—softball games for your biologist colleagues, potluck picnics for your painter acquaintances, retreats for your poet friends—and takes it upon yourself to craft the ceremonies that can turn ordinary events into communions. You may not know exactly how to proceed, but saying things like "Welcome" and "Thank you for coming" and "It's good to see you" make for an excellent beginning. The rest you can learn on the fly as you sponsor more of these gatherings.

Maybe we can have some new festivals. Maybe we can have new book fairs, where writers celebrate one another; new craft fairs, where artisans share their spirit as well as their wares; new film festivals, where distribution deals and the hottest parties are not the only topics of conversation. But this will take your help and your leadership. Are you game?

EXERCISE **52** • *Form a Group*

This is an excellent time to invite a handful of everyday creative people like yourself to meet in a regular and ritual way for some activity. You don't need to create an artists' support group, a writing critique group, or anything of that sort. You could just meet with like-minded others to fix one another's leaky faucets or to sing cowboy songs. You could go out together and protest some indignity like starvation in America, do volunteer work together, or take your children to the ball game. The goals of such gatherings are simple but often elusive: to laugh together and to feel human.

You could start each meeting with a small ceremony—sharing a loaf of good bread and toasting each other's creative spirit with a glass of cider. Then you might busy yourselves with some good, serious fun. What do you think? Is it time to start organizing?

WEEK 27

53. Extend a Tradition

In the last few weeks, you've made some connections with children and with other like-minded creative people. Now I'd like you to think about the connections you can make to the living and dead creators who work or have worked in your tradition.

When I sit down to write, I feel that I'm participating in a long and honorable tradition that goes back thousands of years and includes writers from all over the world. Many of these writers never saw their work published, but we have labored in the same fields. To be honest, I feel more connected to them than to my courtyard neighbors or even my psychotherapist colleagues. I like to think that you are getting a little bit of Dostoyevsky and a little bit of Camus through me, because they and others like them reside in my being. My participation in the writing tradition enriches me and, if this book is of value to you, it enriches you too.

> *The secret is to follow the advice the masters give you in their works while doing something different in yours.*
>
> — EDGAR DEGAS

Not long ago, a blocked painter named Joe came in to see me. He was tired of his current painting style and wanted to try something new. But the ideas he found himself toying with—a series of Japanese eggplant paintings, scenes of a ruined barn, a Miró-esque fantasy made up of certain personal symbols—didn't impress him much. He could picture the finished products and he liked them well enough, but he didn't love them. Something was missing but he couldn't identify what.

We sat down with a pile of art books. I wanted him to refresh his memory about the history of art and to reconnect with paintings that had once inspired him. Many of the paintings we looked at that day he neither liked nor admired. Some that he admired nevertheless failed to speak to him. Some paintings seemed wonderful for their time but not significant today. Joe respectfully put all those aside and flagged only the ones that moved him.

We ended up with the works of seven painters arrayed in front of us. (For those of you familiar with art history and curious to know Joe's choices, they were Chaim Soutine, Nathan Oliveira, Alice Neel, Edvard Munch, Amadeo Modigliani, Alberto Giacometti, and Francis Bacon.) I didn't ask Joe to articulate what he thought

> *The talent of each artist is the result of his own inspiration and his own study of past tradition.*
>
> — GUSTAVE COURBET

these painters had in common, though the fact that each of them distorted the human form seemed a likely thread. I asked him instead to wordlessly study these paintings and to arrive, if he could, at a new sense of what he wanted to paint. He looked at the paintings, shut his eyes, and then opened them after a moment.

He said that he wanted to reconnect with New York City, where he grew up, and with the human figure, which he hadn't painted in more than a decade. He saw a subway platform, an express train whizzing by, and the distorted images of commuters on the platform reflected in the windows of the passing train. Those images commingled with the distorted images of passengers in the train. He understood that this painting was quite ambitious and technically difficult, and that it also bordered on a cliché, and yet something about it moved him deeply. He had to try his hand at it.

Extending a tradition means connecting with the efforts of other artists for the sake of arriving at your own truth. It doesn't mean adopting their lifestyle, personality, or bad habits. Joe didn't have to drink like the alcoholic Soutine, experience Oliveira's depressions, or commit suicide like Modigliani. But what was on their canvases spoke to him, and served to put him in touch with what he wanted to say as a painter.

EXERCISE 53 • *Surround Yourself with Fellow Artists*

Name one person in your tradition. If you're a singer, that might be a singer, songwriter, or musician. Write down that person's name in capital letters on a sheet of paper: say, PATSY CLINE. Put Patsy up on the refrigerator. Name another person in your tradition. Write down that person's name in capital letters: say, TAMMY WYNETTE. Paste Tammy to the inside of your guitar case. Name another five or ten practitioners of your art and put them up around you, on your bathroom mirror, along the walls of your hall, on the ceiling above your bed. Whenever you encounter these names, stop for a second. Think of their work fondly. Remind yourself that you and they share a tradition, one your creative efforts extend and enrich.

You might also do the kind of work that Joe and I did together. You might, for instance, reread the famous articles in your field or visit some local museums. By doing so, you'll reconnect with your traditions and propel yourself forward.

WEEK 27

54. Get Lost in the Landscape

My first drawing class shocked me. I loved ideas, not objects like ferns and bushes, and I hardly expected that going out with a sketch pad into nature would be pleasant. In fact, it turned out to be much more. It was a radical, transformative experience to sit quietly, not smoking (back then, I smoked two and a half packs of cigarettes a day), not imposing my will on the landscape, not caught up in ego or accomplishment, but just looking, seeing, and transcribing. For perhaps the first time ever, I sat for hours paying attention to the world outside of me.

> *The idea is to have no idea. Get lost. Get lost in the landscape.*
> — MALCOLM MORLEY

How tiny the objects on my sketch pad looked! For a big-headed person, it was strange, disconcerting, and then revelatory to realize that if I transcribed what I saw just as I saw it, each object in right relationship to its neighbors, the result felt right to the eye and good to the heart. I learned that you didn't have to start with the mind. You could start with reality instead. This lesson stayed with me when I counseled clients in therapy or sat down to write. Having sat with nature, I could be more real.

If we picture a tree in our mind, we make it very large, because it occupies the whole of our mind frame. If we then transcribe that mental image of a tree onto the page, we end up with a gigantic tree that seems to be the only thing in existence. Our idea of a tree has overwhelmed reality. But if we go out into our backyard and look around, we'll see that even the grandest tree has a modesty about it, because of the presence of its neighbors and the vastness of the horizon. This is the special reality testing you get to engage in when you lose yourself in the landscape around you.

Sketching outdoors gave me a glimpse of a new

awareness state, one different from the trance of writing that I already knew intimately. With writing, the focus always remained inward. It was almost as if I wrote with my eyes shut. But while sketching I had to keep my eyes open. I had to process sights while maintaining a quiet mind. What I learned from this experience proved valuable in my work with clients, where I also had to process information in a "no mind" way, and in my everyday creative life, which required that I take in data from the world without forcing it to match my preconceptions.

> When you go out to paint, try to forget what objects are before you. Merely think, here is a little square of blue, here is a streak of yellow, and paint it all exactly until it yields your own naive impression of the scene.
>
> — CLAUDE MONET

Your chances of creating deeply hinge on the quality of your awareness state. You've worked on this already in earlier sections when you got anxious calmly, wrestled with your demons, and roused out of dream sleep. Ordinary awareness is too hectic and noisy for creativity. Getting lost in the landscape is one of the best ways to leave ordinary awareness behind and achieve an awareness state where connections get made with no effort whatsoever. You may be sketching the landscape; but because of the excellent quiet you maintain, you may also be finding the perfect conclusion for your novel or the solution to your computer problems at work.

EXERCISE 54A • *Get Lost in the Landscape*

Whether or not your creative outlet is the visual arts, I'd love you to experience sketching outdoors and losing yourself in the landscape. No other feeling is quite like it. You'll need a few basic artist's tools: a sketch pad, pencils, an eraser, maybe a box of charcoals, maybe a folding chair. You don't need an easel; you don't need paints or brushes. You don't need anything fancy or special. Getting lost in the landscape couldn't be easier.

I invite you to wander out into the countryside. Just stop anywhere, sit down, look, and begin to draw. See how small the faraway trees are. Draw them. As you draw, notice how quiet your mind gets. In a minute or two you'll vanish, entranced. You'll feel connected to the world around you and to your deepest self. The goal of this exercise is not to have you become a nature painter but to experience the awareness state that arises when you sit down in the middle of nature, look, and draw.

EXERCISE 54B • *Get Lost in Your Own Home*

You can achieve this same awareness state and reap the same benefits of sketching quietly outdoors while in your own house or apartment. You might sketch the view out your bedroom window or the plants arrayed on the sill above your kitchen sink. Choose a subject, open your sketch pad, look, and draw.

Let go of any preconceived ideas. You might pose yourself a question about your current creative project, hoping to answer it in the quiet state you achieve when you sketch, but once you pose it, let it go. Just look and draw. Lose yourself in your own home.

55. Picture Your Audience

About a dozen years ago, I had dinner with a literary agent who was thinking about representing a nonfiction book of mine that had to do with artists in therapy. But although he was considering handling the proposal, he was nevertheless unhappy with it, because he felt I'd failed to identify my audience. Was the book intended for therapists? For young artists? For mid-career artists? For people interested in creativity? Sometimes I addressed one audience and sometimes another. That really wouldn't do. He lectured me about the necessity of having a clear picture of my audience and writing the book for them and no one else.

> *Potential audiences are real people found in real places.*
>
> — SUZANNE LACY

I listened. What he was saying suddenly clicked. Like every writer I'd heard this admonition before. It was as standard a piece of advice as "write about what you know" and "show, don't tell." But I'd never taken it to heart. If occasionally I did think about who might want to read one of my books, I simply designated as my audience "any smart person interested in what I'm interested in." I could even name members of that audience: my friends with whom I talked about the things I wrote about. If they were interested in what I had to say, wasn't that a sufficient sign that other people might be interested?

The answer to that question turned out to be "no." It wasn't a sufficient sign. I had to actually picture my audience and take their needs and desires seriously if I wanted to write books that were correctly targeted. And if I wanted many readers, then I had to craft my material in such a way that I spoke to a broad spectrum of the reading public who had three million titles to choose from and space on their bedside table for one or two books. How to do that and still say what I wanted to say became a question that fascinated me.

It's always a tricky question: to what extent should you consider the wants of your audience, rather than focusing on the imperatives of your work? It's possible—even likely—that if you care too much about garnering a large audience you'll start pandering and not tell the truth as you know it. What if you know for sure that most people want happy endings and prefer blue to yellow? Then you'll be tempted to create victorious heroes and paintings with more sky than sun. What if you know for sure that they love melody, that they always have and always will? How likely will you be to try your hand at dissonance?

> *Who is the public now that it has changed color?*
> — JUDITH BACA

But the reverse can also be true. You may write thick, unyielding sentences if you write for your ear only. You may doom yourself to a lifetime in a corporate mail room if you compose nothing but duets for tin whistle and bongo. Mustn't it be wise to aim for some popularity, just as you'd aim to make popular sandwiches at your deli or popular cars at your factory? Isn't the customer, if not always right, certainly always the customer?

These are difficult, important questions. One proof of how large they loom is how nervous it makes most of us to think about them. One cure for this anxiety is to make the effort to picture potential members of your audience. By picturing the people who might appreciate your work, you give yourself the chance to learn what they really want and what you, in turn, really want to provide.

EXERCISE 55 • *Start an Audience Wall*

Begin to picture your potential audience. Who actually comes to modern string quartet concerts? Who attends such concerts in New York, Paris, Omaha, and Berkeley? Who buys modern string quartet CDs? Could children be interested in them? Put up a few smiling children and think about how to reach them. Could folks in Memphis be interested? Maybe you might add some jazz and a little country to your next quartet. Could poker players in Canarsie be interested? Not at first glance, but their grandparents in Vienna were. Could a love of classical music have been passed through the genes? Look through magazines for photos of people whom you imagine might like what you create. Cut out those photos and tape them to your wall.

Put up lots of pictures. Study them. Maybe they'll have very little to say to you. Maybe your wall of pictures will sadden you, as you think about how difficult it is to sell what you produce. Maybe you'll find it dismaying to think about reaching such a disparate group of people. On the other hand, maybe you'll get some new ideas and insights. Maybe you'll see that men might also be interested in the novel you're writing or that your listening audience is younger than you imagined. Study these faces. I have a guarantee for you: one of them will look you right in the eye and change the way you think about your audience.

56. Connect with People

Some very creative people have been recluses, happy to do their creative work in isolation and unwilling to relate to others. But these same recluses have also tended to suffer from severe depression and other emotional problems. So while it may feel natural to devote yourself to your creative work and succumb to feelings of separation and alienation, it nevertheless isn't a terrific idea in terms of your overall happiness and health. In our religion, we prize creativity but we also prize an all-around mentally sound way of being that includes relationships of all sorts, ones that we actively seek out and nurture.

> *Why should it happen that among all the people, the great many women whom I see and am fond of, suddenly somebody I meet for half an hour opens the door into poetry?*
> — MAY SARTON

Over the past weeks we've talked about relating to children, to members of your audience, to an art buddy, and to nature. Here I'd like you to think about relating to:

- colleagues
- marketplace players
- friends interested in your creative efforts
- family members who might be invited to learn more about your work
- other human beings worth knowing

Imagine adding these people to your life. If that seems like a good idea, start the ball rolling by making a list of the interesting people you know whom you haven't talked to in a long time. Call up or E-mail one or two of them. Is there a special friend from college you haven't communicated with in twenty years? A writer you met at a conference whom you liked a lot and who gave you her card but whom you never got around to contacting? A painter you exhibited with at a group show ten years ago? A chemist you met at a conference in Moscow some years back who shares your love of polymers and Baroque music? Make the small effort it would take to contact one or two such people.

The soloist can emerge only after having participated in the group dance.

— ARSHILE GORKY

You might also want to craft a plan to meet new people. Maybe it's time to attend that local writers' conference where editors, agents, and writers gather. Maybe it's the right moment to drop a line to two or three top people in your field, telling them what you admire about their work and inviting them to get to know you. Maybe it would be a good idea to send an E-mail to some of your colleagues and ask them over for a networking breakfast. Many of the things you might try in this regard are free and simple. Not much more is required than the courage to connect and relate.

You will have to go it alone when you create. But that doesn't mean that you shouldn't garner support for your work, be supportive of others, and know many people in a simple, human way. You don't have to invite them over for dinner every third day or throw them huge parties. All you have to do is pay attention and be considerate when you interact with them. People aren't an imposition—as corny as it sounds, they are your brothers and sisters. You'll be very pleased to have them in your life when the novel you're writing is published and they attend your first book signing or when your painting career is stalled and one of them calls to tell you about an opportunity that suits you miraculously well.

EXERCISE 56 • *Walk Blind with a Friend Beside You*

Find a partner for this exercise. You might call up an old friend or use this exercise to deepen your friendship with a new one.

Go with your partner to a park, a college campus, or an open spot in the woods. Have your partner blindfold you. The two of you then head out, you on your blind adventure, she watching that you don't fall off a cliff or walk into a plateglass window. Your partner should stay close enough to protect you but should also maintain her distance, so that you can experience your blindness. Your goals are to practice moving forward without benefit of sight and to entrust your safety to another person.

At first you may not want to move. Then you'll step out gingerly. Soon you'll become more confident. You'll feel the warmth of the sun on your face and the warmth of being protected by another person. In this way, you can learn about surrender; you can listen; and you can explore. At the same time, you can be intimate with another human being.

Switch places. Watch out for your friend. Now she is blind and has put her trust in you. Earn it.

PART 8

Be Ambitious

Weeks 29-32

57. Want Everything

The desire to make our mark, to do great work, and to create like a god are immodesties that are nothing to fear. Desire and creativity are intimately related, and the most creative person is also the person who longs for it the most and chases after it the most. Do you want to be called an important twenty-first century painter? Good. Do you want to have an intellectual movement named after you? Excellent. The movies we cherish and the breakthrough drugs that save our lives are not created by people whose only desires are to nap and retire early. Our geniuses are also our kings and queens of desire.

For the next month, your focus will be on dreaming big and letting your innate ambitiousness out of the bag. Most of us stifle our feelings of ambitiousness, sometimes because we think we have no chance of getting what we want, sometimes because we think it's unseemly to desire so much. Maybe we doubt that we really have it in us to accomplish great things; maybe our first creative efforts are so weak that we're inclined to quit. Such powerful blockers make us exile our desire to some underground cell, where it turns to sadness and despair. My invitation to you is to free your desire from that underground cell. Welcome it back. Want again.

Let's directly address our worries about wanting. The first and most insistent is: what chance do I have? What chance do I have of making a breakthrough in painting? Only a handful of people in the history of the world have done truly groundbreaking work. What chance do I have to make a big blockbuster movie? Only a handful of people get to do that, and even they have to make movies aimed at teenagers, it seems. What's the point of going out and taking photographs with my old-fashioned camera in the middle of a digital revolution? How smart is that? What's the point of writing a novel when it's so hard to get one published these days? Why voluntarily run into that brick wall?

If we allow ourselves to want in the face of such long odds, aren't we setting ourselves up for bitter disappointment? Yes, we are. And don't we know from philosophies like Buddhism to let go of earthly desires in order to avoid the suffering that comes with attachment? Yes, we do. Aren't our loftiest goals almost unreachable? Yes, they are. Well, then? "Well,

> *I'm glad I want everything in the world—good and bad—bitter and sweet—I want it all.*
> — GEORGIA O'KEEFFE

then, what?" an everyday creative person replies. It is still our nature and our destiny to want what we want. Put skin cells in a nutrient culture and they make skin. Put nerve cells in a culture and they make an embryonic nervous system. Put human beings on this earth and they want what human beings want: to use their brain, to discover new things, to live authentically, all of which together amount to a desire to create.

Not only should you unfetter your desire: you should unleash it in the service of good and grand projects. Create a device that neutralizes nuclear warheads or that cleans the ocean of waste and debris. Use painting to make a whole generation feel deeply and recognize their common humanity. Use language to expose a horrible injustice. Want everything; but to be more precise about it, want everything true, beautiful, and good.

When you create a masterpiece and everyone hails it as such, take your bows modestly. But you and I will both know how much you wanted the ac-claim. You and I will both know that you've been writing your Nobel prize acceptance speech since you were nine. You and I will both know, though we don't have to admit it to anyone, how absurdly large are our fantasies, appetites, and dreams. I know that about you and you know that about me. It's one of the laws of our religion, about which we have nothing to be embarrassed.

> *Each day I discover still more beautiful things; it's enough to drive me mad. I want to do everything so much: my head is bursting with it.*
>
> — CLAUDE MONET

EXERCISE 57 • *Write a Letter About What You Want . . . And What You Will Do to Get It*

Write a letter to yourself. Begin with "I want . . ." Name the things that you want: fame, glory, brilliant works, adulation, self-satisfaction, publicity, a second home in Italy, immortality.

Then put down what you'll do to get all this. "In order to make my twelve Academy Award–winning films, I will . . ." This might include working twelve hours a day, not two or three, on the student film you're making; tacking up affirmations on the bath-room mirror, even though you find the idea of affir-mations a little silly; and learning what film some director you love is making next so as to be a part of it, even as his dog walker or cellphone recharger. This should be the longer part of the letter, full of bright ideas and excellent self-instruction.

Want everything. Then plan how to get it.

58. Demand Grandeur

We associate grandeur with events like royal weddings and sights like the Grand Canyon. Hotels are grand, canals are grand, cruise ships are grand. But something about that way of thinking prevents us from demanding grandeur from the other stuff of existence, like a sentence we craft, a jam we concoct, or a kiss we give. For more reasons than we can count, grandeur isn't very present in our daily lives.

> *All important things in art have always originated from the deepest feeling about the mystery of Being.*
> — MAX BECKMANN

In all the meetings I've ever attended—faculty meetings, business meetings, meetings of therapists, meetings of writers—I've never heard anyone say, "What's wanted is a little more grandeur." Have you? On the long list of things discussed when people gather, grandeur never appears. There are no parties honoring it, no organizations devoted to it, no lobbyists button-holing members of Congress and whispering, "Support the grandeur bill and we'll make it worth your while!"

At this moment, I'm sitting in a sterile coffee-break room in a suite of offices, writing by hand before the class I teach begins. In a corner of the room are some boxes of computer parts. There's a Pepsi machine. A microwave. A copy machine. A fire extinguisher. A sink. A wastepaper basket. A metal cabinet for office supplies. The walls of the room are blue-gray. The round table I'm sitting at is blue-gray. The floor is blue-gray. The chairs at the table are blue-gray. But on the wall across from me is a poster of a Manuel Neri oil-on-paper sketch called *Alberica No. 1*. It portrays a woman with a blue face, a yellow torso, and burgundy legs. The top half of the background is brilliant yellow and the bottom half is a striking blue. If I didn't have it or something like it on the wall to look at, I would surely die of grandeur deprivation in a room like this.

> *One paints from nature not in order to copy, but to express feelings of grandeur.*
> — GEORGES VANTONGERLOO

Think about your own life. What last stirred feelings of grandeur in you? Was it something you saw on the commute to work or something you experienced at a meeting? Probably not. My hunch is that you were last stirred by music, film, or a passage in a book. You stopped, listened to the music, and said to yourself "How beautiful" or "How powerful" or "This is good stuff!" You were transported. In the back of your mind you whispered, "I should be creating." You said to yourself, but maybe not in a way that you could hear the message clearly, "Without this beauty I would die."

Without a Neri on the wall, or Mozart in the air, or Tolstoy in our hands, we would wither away, no matter how good our benefits and stock options at work. We need grandeur to survive, and as everyday creative people it is up to us to supply it for ourselves and for others. But we forget our possibilities and our responsibilities. We forget that we are potentially grand creatures who have it in us to create. We forget that grandeur is available and that we can create it ourselves. Our objective for the next few days is to remind ourselves that as everyday creative people we are obliged to produce grand work—work that really moves us.

EXERCISE **58A** • *Write Some Grand Sentences*

Today, write some grand sentences and begin a grand piece of writing. Do this even if you're a biologist or a business executive and not a professional writer.

By grand sentences I don't mean pretentious, stylish, or clever sentences. I mean sentences that are true, good, and beautiful. Once you have a first sentence written, however long that takes, write a second, then a third. Continue on until you have a whole grand paragraph.

Maybe that will take you hours. Maybe you'll run out of time today and not finish. In that case, begin again tomorrow and write more grand sentences. Continue on until you have a grand short story, article, or essay. Then share the grandeur: submit your piece for publication.

EXERCISE **58B** • *Keep Grandeur Handy*

Many people keep a small object like a rabbit's foot around for good luck. Let's start a tradition in our religion where we keep an object nearby that reminds us that we intend to produce grand work.

If you're a writer (even if you use a computer exclusively) get yourself a beautiful pen and carry it around with you. If you're an anthropologist, put a totem on your key chain from a culture that fascinates you. Find some resonant object that, whenever you encounter it in your pocket, reminds you that it is a joy—and also your obligation—to do grand work.

59. Aim for a Response

Am I creating solely for me? Or do I want to touch you? It would be very ambitious of me to imag-ine that I can generate a response

A color is as strong as the impression it creates.

— IVAN ALBRIGHT

in you, that I can stop you in your tracks and have you exclaim, "Wow, that was interesting!" But I am exactly that ambitious, and so is everyone else who believes in this religion of ours. Not only do we want you to know that a certain in-justice exists—we want you to rage against it. Not only do we want you to know that the distant moun-tains can be rendered blue—we want to thrill you with our depiction. We want everything, including especially that you be transformed by our work.

It's fine to want fame, to launch a project simply because some puzzle or question interests you, or to create for any one of many other reasons. But at the end of the day, the most important reason to create— and a prime reason why creativity can be a religion— is that by creating you affect other people. You can make them morally better, more knowledgeable, more sensitive to their environment, and smarter consumers, citizens, or human beings. You can make them laugh at their foibles, empathize with their fel-low creatures, or shout in outrage. You can change lives by creating.

For me, Stanley Milgram's work is in this cate-gory of creativity. Milgram, a Yale professor with World War II and the Holocaust on his mind, won-dered what would happen if he invited ordinary people into a lab setting and asked them to act as "teacher" to a "learner" who was a predetermined confederate of the experimenters. Milgram advised his unsuspecting subjects that they would have to administer electric shock to the learner whenever he answered a question incorrectly and that they would need to keep raising the voltage each time the learner failed—even, as it turned out, after the learner appeared to suffer a heart attack.

Anything that is written to please the author is worthless.
— BLAISE PASCAL

Psychiatrists surveyed beforehand agreed that very few subjects would be willing to administer any shock at all and that none would go to the very end of the voltage scale. But in fact, just about every subject acting as "teacher" administered the maximum shock possible. Some of them protested while doing so and a few genuinely seemed to want to stop, but virtually none of them actually stopped. Egged on by a man in a white lab coat, these good citizens had no trouble torturing their neighbors.

Milgram ran this experiment on obedience to verify a hunch he had about human nature. He suspected that we are very dangerous creatures beneath our civilized surface and that it would take little inducement—just an experimenter saying "You must proceed"—for most people to administer heart-stopping electric shock to a fellow human being. His hunch turned out to be true to an astonishing extent, reminding us that horrors are lurking not just in Nazi Germany or in the Balkans, but in every contemporary heart.

Did Milgram set out to affect us? I bet he did— I bet he meant us to be struck by the implications of his research. Like Milgram, we want our audience to feel something and to learn something from our creative efforts. Sometimes we pursue a scientific puzzle just because it's of intellectual interest; sometimes we want our film to be a box-office hit. But this is not us at our best. Our greater ambition is to move hearts and open minds. If you stop and articulate what audience response you're aiming for, you'll get a clearer sense of your own values and give yourself the chance to choose projects most in line with those values.

EXERCISE 59 • *Explain Your Intentions to Yourself*

Spend some time over the next few days explaining to yourself what sort of response you hope people will have to your work and deciding whether that response is really what you're after. If it isn't, you will need to change what you create and the very way you think about creating. For instance:

- Is your work ironic? Do you want your audience to wink knowingly?
- Is your work clever? Do you want your audience to applaud your mental dexterity?
- Is your work entertaining? Do you want people to choose your novel to take with them to the beach this summer?
- Is your work angry? Do you want people to share your outrage?

Devote yourself for the next few days to this exercise and learn what responses you hope to elicit from your audience.

60. Play the Tallest Queen in History

Everyday creative people think that they can go on stage and make audiences see them as tall, even if they happen to be short. They presume that, despite their very human limitations, they can write symphonies that the gods themselves would gather to play. They imagine that, despite the progress we've already made, they can take astronomy or computer technology another step forward. They may lack confidence twelve different ways, but they are confident in this one regard, that they have it in them to create.

A client of mine painted and also worked with disturbed children as a clinical art therapist. She came to see me because she'd stopped painting and because her career felt stalled. Her negative self-talk and lack of confidence became quickly apparent. Inside she was saying things like "I'm not good enough" and "I'm not brave enough" and "I can't dream that big." I had her dispute those ideas. I had her say new things, some as simple as "I can." During the course of our work together, we fought a pitched battle against her inner demons. I can't say whether or not we fully exorcised them, but we ended our work together on a hopeful note.

This client called me a few weeks ago and told me that in the three years since we'd last met she'd become the president of her local art therapy association, presented a clinical paper at a small art therapy conference and then at the national conference, been invited to teach a course in art therapy at a prestigious university, and started painting big and bold. She was thrilled and so was I.

She had given herself permission to think big. Allowing yourself to think big—to imagine that you can add something of real importance to your field of study, to suppose that you can write a novel that will affect people deeply, to feel certain that the message you hope to communicate in your music is vital for people to hear—is the kind of ambitiousness that characterizes everyday creative people. To imagine that you could make the subject of your paintings light itself, as Monet did, is an example of thinking big. To imagine that you could invent calculus because you needed it to continue your work on celestial mechanics, as Newton did, is an example of thinking big.

> *At the age of six I wanted to be a cook. At seven I wanted to be Napoleon. And my ambition has been growing steadily ever since.*
>
> — SALVADOR DALI

The playwright David Hare had the idea of writing a play in the form of an extended monologue. Such an idea is ambitious enough, but Hare had a greater ambition. He wanted to perform the monologue himself. He'd never acted and didn't know if he could act, but he believed what all everyday creative people believe: there's no harm in trying. He went to a director colleague, who assured him that he could be taught to act. Hare learned what he needed to learn and went on to give successful performances of his own play-length monologue. Can you think that large?

EXERCISE **60** • *Think Big*

What would help you think big? Most people can't answer this question. They don't know what inner movement would allow them to see themselves as equal to any creative task, to start mapping out enormous projects, to view themselves as the potential stars in their field. If they do answer, they say things like "Maybe I need to find more time" or "Maybe I need to recover from my early psychological traumas." But the right answer is, "I must surrender to my own greatness."

> *Short as I am, I played the tallest queen in history. I thought tall, I felt tall—and I looked tall.*
>
> — HELEN HAYES

Obstacles like a lack of time or a problematic past are real. But still the main task is surrender: surrender to a way of conceiving yourself as great, capable, special, big. Such a way of thinking is radically different from our ordinary self-conception. Usually we feel most comfortable thinking of ourselves as, if not ordinary, as only potentially great but not actually great.

But it would be wonderful if you could say, "I surrender. I am great. I am!" So today, affirm your own greatness. Say, "I am great!" Murmur it all day long. There is nothing else for you to "do," although, after you say "I am great" enough times, you may feel compelled to think big and start an enormous creative project. Let go of the image of yourself as ordinary or only potentially great, and surrender to this new self-image, of you equal to playing the tallest queen in history—equal even to changing the course of history. Think that big and feel that great.

WEEK 31

61. Change Radically

Many people feel stalled in their career or creative outlet but unequal to the task of changing radically. Indeed, it is an act of great ambition and courage to change radically. What you are asserting when you make a radical change—say, from being an accountant to being a painter, from being a sculptor to being a weaver, from being an actor to being a performance artist—is that, despite any difficulties you may encounter, you intend to go in the direction your wisdom and deep desires lead you. You courageously assert this even though you may not really know which way to turn or have much of an idea of the consequences in store for you.

> *Even to think about changing something that seems so basic gives you a pain in the stomach!*
>
> — NELL BLAINE

The biggest change in my life, creatively speaking, came when I switched from writing fiction to nonfiction. That change saved my life. My fiction wasn't wanted but my nonfiction was. Editors continued to ignore my novels but began to buy my self-help books. Instead of having to duck questions about what I did, I could relish answering: "Oh, I write. What? Oh, yes. I'm published." Instead of feeling as if I had no creative outlet, I again had a place to put my thoughts and feelings. I am not exaggerating when I say that this change was lifesaving.

But I had no idea that I should make this lifesaving switch. I had no premonition, no plan, no insight, no intuition. I only knew that some change was in order. I gave up fiction, became a therapist, gave a few lectures, a book idea emerged, then a book proposal—and, seven years after quitting fiction, I found myself writing nonfiction. If you'd asked me in 1980, "Why don't you give up novels and do something else?" I'd have replied, "That would kill me!" By 1985, believing that my writing life was behind me, my reply would have been, "I'm done with fiction. Let somebody else bang his head there." In

1990, signing my first nonfiction book contract, I'd have murmured, "Life is a very strange journey."

As was the case with me, you may have no idea what ambitious change you want or need to make. But you may also have the clear sense that some radical change is needed, perhaps because you're not happy with the creative work you're currently doing, perhaps because you're having too hard a

> *Do not ask me who I am and do not ask me to remain the same.*
> — MICHEL FOUCAULT

time selling what you produce. If that feels like the case, try your hand at the following exercise. It may aim you in the right direction.

EXERCISE 61 • *Contemplate a Radical Change*

Write the autobiography of your creative life. You'll find that even if you don't need to make any radical changes right now, writing this creative autobiography is useful and will help you explain your work to others, which you will need to do when it comes time to show it and sell it.

The autobiography of your creative life might look something like the following hypothetical (and very brief) one:

> I've loved stone since I was a boy. To this day, primitive stone figures from all over the world thrill me. When I grew up, I knew I wanted to work with stone, not with wood, glass, or iron, or anything but stone. But even so, when I thought I wanted to be an artist I started out painting, not sculpting, mainly because painting classes were easier to find in the small town where I lived. But I really hated the give of canvas, so after a couple of years I switched from canvas to masonite. But

painting on masonite wasn't the answer. Finally I "came home" to stone! The first few years I carved animals, but then I moved on to faces. I think I'll love faces until I die, but right now I feel they're a little played out in me. I've been toying with a few new ideas, but actually I feel stuck and don't know what I want to do next.

Refine your creative autobiography until it feels as truthful as you can make it. If you're lucky, it will be several pages long and full of insights that surprise you. Read it over. Then ask yourself, "What would constitute a radical change?" Might it be switching from stone to wood? From representative sculpture to abstract sculpture? What clues can you find in your autobiography to help you solve the mystery of where to turn next, if you happen to be stuck right now?

If an idea comes to you, try it out. It may seem bizarre to switch from stone to wood when wood repulses you, but think how horrible writing nonfiction sounded to me twenty years ago. So who can say? Squander a day on a radical change. You can always go back to the work you're currently doing, and maybe the change you've experimented with will turn out to be just what the doctor ordered.

WEEK 31

62. Exhaust Yourself

Last night I was feeling blue about my lack of productivity and my unwillingness to exhaust myself in the service of my writing. I took a shower and in the shower reminded myself that I'd written two dozen or more books in the past twenty-eight years and that a number that large was surely some sign of productivity. But I didn't convince myself, because I knew that on some of those books I hadn't worked hard enough. If I'd wanted to excuse myself, I could have produced a list of plausible reasons why this book or that book fell short, but I didn't have any stomach for that exercise. I preferred to let the hot water tumble down on the truth, that, like so many people, I hadn't fought the good fight often enough.

> *I am beginning to think that by the time Whistler had worked for sixty-two sittings on that portrait they tell about, he would have been a pretty unlucky devil if he hadn't hit something fairly good in all that slaving on the same thing.*
>
> — GEORGIA O'KEEFFE

The only answer, for me and for you, is to try harder to honor our ambitions and our obligations. But maybe you aren't ready to take those vows. Maybe you have doubts about the wisdom of exhausting yourself in the service of your creative work. Maybe you think you'll be visited by Beethoven's bouts of nervous irritability or Dostoyevsky's anxiety attacks. These are legitimate worries, because devoting yourself to your creative work can take its toll on your physical and psychological well-being. But there are better reasons to commit to making the effort: that this is *your* time on earth, *your* chance to create worthy things, *your* opportunity to conceive a startling idea when, seconds before, nothing had existed.

Many religions demand arduous practices from their flock, like circumcisions, fasts, or confessions. But it is for the clergy class of each religion that the hardest practices are reserved. As a member of the clergy, you may be asked never to marry, never to have children, never to own any worldly possessions, never to speak except in praise of God. In our religion of creativity, each of us is a member of the clergy class. We are each penitent and priest. Shouldn't we demand of ourselves that we be as religious in our own way as any monk or priest? Is it too much to ask that we exhaust ourselves in the service of our creativity, since we are our religion's leaders as well as its practitioners?

> *My painting studio is in downtown Los Angeles, near Little Tokyo. I work until I'm exhausted.*
> — MICHAEL TODD

If the only reason you have for trekking across the desert is that it occurred to you to try, the obstacles the desert presents are bound to wear you out in short order. But if you are trekking across the desert because you are on a vision quest or because you want to prove to yourself that you can, then the obstacles are part of the process and you have a real chance of making it to the next oasis. If you begin writing a short story because you have an idea for a short story, when you don't know what words to put down next you'll stop writing. But if you begin writing a short story because you have an idea for a short story *and* because you are a priestess in the religion of creativity, then when you stall you'll take a deep breath, make some popcorn or take a shower, and get back to work.

If you think of creativity as a religion, if that metaphor feels apt and useful to you, then you'll also feel encouraged to work longer hours at your creative projects and use up more adrenaline in their service. You'll find yourself saying, "Why shouldn't I exhaust myself at my songwriting? Isn't this my life's work?" You'll find yourself becoming a more devoted creator.

EXERCISE **62** • *Exhaust Yourself*

Tomorrow, take the day off from work and exhaust yourself in the service of a really big idea. If you can't take the day off, wait until the weekend to do this exercise.

Start at sunrise and go until midnight, getting tired, confused, crazy, anxious, frayed, sad, depressed, and whatever else befalls you as you struggle to realize this big idea of yours. When, after several hours of doing battle, you can't muster another thought, then scream, cry, beat your head against the wall, take a walk, take a bath, take a nap, brush the cat, do anything you like, but do not even think about throwing in the towel.

Outline a whole book in this one day. Write that scene without which your novel can't get moving. Paint the painting that defines your genre, the painting you've been meaning to start for years. Write the song that sums up your generation. Even if you can't reach one of these lofty goals, making an effort of this sort is remarkable and courageous and deserves a reward. So exhaust yourself and then reward yourself, at the very least with the compliment, "I worked hard, I didn't fall apart, and I'm proud that I tried."

WEEK 32

63. Build a World

A young woman from the projects goes into urban planning as a career because she'd love to see new, better cities created, ones powered by the sun and free of prejudice. A young man becomes a theater director not to have Broadway hits but because Greek drama has gotten under his skin and he can envision staging Sophocles in modern dress. A woman champions preventative medicine, because in her mind's eye she can see a healthier world; a man joins the Peace Corps because he can picture crops growing in the desert. These everyday creative people are hungry to build the worlds that their minds have already envisioned.

Are these naive, utopian ambitions? Are they romantic and unrealistic? Maybe. But we support them with all our heart. Reality may deal each of these ambitions a terrific blow, but still much excellent work may get done. If you have the ambition to build a world, creative people everywhere support you in your dream. We love it when our colleagues come to us and say "I see a new way of using the Internet for good" or "I can picture a new kind of kinetic sculpture." We love it when our friends obsess about new ideas, rather than their usual worries. We love it when our creative congregation adopts as its motto, "I can envision and make new worlds."

> Though I have considerable interest in Europe and in traveling, I am most content with simply working and allowing the world that I'm creating to unfold before my eyes.
>
> — NATHAN OLIVEIRA

You can also build worlds completely in your mind. Can't travel to Venice this year? Build yourself a Venice-of-the-mind and visit there. Whenever you need a lively new world to inhabit, just create one. Everyday creative people can mind-travel whenever they like. Are you sitting in your living room with no place to go? Picture your hometown and tell yourself a story about the Johnsons, the family who used to live next door. Tired of working too far above the ground, on the twentieth floor of a highrise, at your day job? Dream up a world of earthworms and create some down-in-the-dirt adventures. To build mind worlds of this sort you need no permits or easements. All you need is your imagination.

> *When I want to read a good book, I write one.*
> — BENJAMIN DISRAELI

Why do so few people do this? Maybe they fear they'll conjure up nightmare worlds. Maybe they have strong injunctions against daydreaming. Maybe their brain cells are preoccupied with the business of surviving. Whatever the reasons, it's a crying shame. Remember the stories you told yourself in childhood, about hidden treasures in the backyard and fantastic trips down the Yukon River? Did those stories take much effort to conjure up? Certainly not. Wouldn't it be nice to sit back and make your life richer right now with some mind travel? Wouldn't it be nice to tell yourself some excellent stories as you drift off to sleep? These, then, are the twin ambitions to hold: to make new worlds that are actual, like books and antibiotics, and to make mind worlds for your own pleasure and enrichment.

If your ambition is to create a model city, a novel of enormous scope, or a new paradigm for occupational medicine or for the symphony, transforming your vision from mind to matter may confound and exhaust you. Yes, you can picture Alice, but can you write her escapades in Wonderland? Yes, you can picture your model city; but who will invite you to build it? The distance between your dream and its fruition can be enormous. But I hope that your reaction to this possibility is the same as mine: "I'll try anyway." This is your time on earth. Is there some other work you'd rather be doing?

EXERCISE **63** • *Imagine a World*

Pick up *The Dictionary of Imaginary Places,* an encyclopedia of fictional places from the world's myths and stories. (This is a real book that you can find at real and virtual bookstores). Thumb through it and stop where you like. Say you land at Fantippo, a West African kingdom. Your job in this exercise is to create a new world that fits between Fantippo and the next entry, which happens to be Farandoulie, a kingdom near the ruins of Melbourne. You might create a fictional world you call Fapawatame, a hamlet in Georgia where everyone mispronounces the word cruller, making the very idea of mispronunciation absurd. Or you might create a place you call Faquahar, an Arabian oasis where figs dance in the moonlight.

Enjoy yourself. Spend a few days in the place you've imagined. Get to know the natives. Have conversations and adventures. Inhabit this world you've created, and remind yourself that imagining is one ambition you can always realize. Then return to your own creative project; it too is a world ready to be imagined and realized.

WEEK 32

64. Feel Immortal

In the religion of creativity, we spend precious little time debating whether or not the soul is immortal, what heaven might be like and who gets to go there, whether we come back after death as frogs or princes or not at all, or any of the other issues that concern traditional theologians. In this religion of ours, we have a different focus. Our desire is to grow so quiet and to work so deeply that we participate fully in the mystery in which we're embedded. When we manage to do that we feel as if we have merged with the universe; for the duration of that experience we feel immortal. That's immortality enough for an everyday creative person, who

I love to do skies. It must be the old Greek gods Zeus and Apollo stirring within me.

— STEPHEN MANIATTY

tends to doubt that her body, soul, or works last forever and who would rather experience immortality here and now.

Feeling immortal has nothing to do with *being* immortal. Feeling immortal is just a feeling, but it is so profound a feeling that everyday creative people devote their lives to creating so they can experience it regularly. They experience immortality when they create; and they also experience it when they are open in an everyday creative way and able to let eternity pass through them without hindering it. Both in the studio and just out walking, they are struck by their intimate, never-ending connection to the universe.

I remember sitting on a hillside in Korea in the dead of night with an army buddy, the two of us supposedly on guard duty but actually just smoking cigarettes, taking in the night smells from the fields, feeling the air's coldness, and watching the stars. For those several hours, that uncanny feeling of participating as a full player in the mystery of existence wouldn't leave me. A year later I found myself on a hillside outside of Eugene, Oregon, listening to an English-language broadcast from a Cuban radio station, and the same feelings coursed through me. In the first instance I was a platoon sergeant in Korea, in the second an anti-war radical, but both times I felt un-self-consciously timeless, bodiless, and immortal.

What stirs these feelings of immortality in you? For composers, it's music. For astronomers, it's the heavens. For naturalists, it's the woods and the mountains. For filmmakers, it's film. For everyday creative people, it's the subjects they love and also life itself, whether experienced on quiet hillsides or in midtown Manhattan. The more you become a creative person, the more you get to enjoy eternity here and now, when you create and just when you turn the corner.

> *Another real thing! I am not dead yet! I can still call forth a piece of soul and set it down in color, fixed forever.*
>
> — KERI HULME

EXERCISE **64** • *Start a Novel, Feel Immortal*

In an earlier exercise I had you sketch outdoors, whether or not the visual arts was your creative outlet, because I wanted you to experience the awareness state and the sense of connection that come from getting lost in the landscape around you. This week I'd like you to start a novel, whether or not your creative outlet is fiction. You don't have to continue the novel once you've completed the exercise, but I'd like you to try your hand at beginning one. Working on a novel, even for just a few days, will provide you with many opportunities to experience immortality.

What will your novel be about? I'd like you to tell an epic story about present-day America. You'll need a theme, so dream up a quick one. It could be something like "man arrives home after forty years in jail" or "daughter of an insurance salesman and a real estate agent leaves suburbia to spend a summer working on the staff of a moralistic senator."

Picture your characters. Then name them. Describe each in a sentence. "John, 44, insurance salesman, is susceptible to colds and paranoid about going bald." "Mary, 43, shops at Nordstrom and is thinking about studying Italian." "Jean, 19, travels everywhere with two teddy bears and a Gold Mastercard."

These are fine initial descriptions. Now scratch the surface by allowing your characters to speak. Imagine John, then Mary, then Jean coming forward and telling his or her story. Write their monologues down just as they present them. Let them speak without interruption. You'll discover an astounding thing: these characters have depth. As they take turns telling their stories, they'll move you and reveal why you picked them. The whole epic story will begin to unfold. Right beneath the surface of your mind, these characters were waiting for just this opportunity. A little scratch, a little incision, and out they poured.

You'll discover another thing. As you lose yourself in the work, you'll feel immortal. Work on your novel for several days, continue it if you like, and enjoy your moments of union with the universe.

209

PART 9

Be Truthful

Weeks 33-36

65. Show Yourself

Our subject for the next four weeks is truthfulness.

Everyday creative people grow as artists by refining their sense of truthfulness and by doing an ever-better job of communicating their truth. If they are chemists working on a new theory, they don't ignore the journal article on their desk that may refute their ideas. They take it into account, however difficult that feels. If they are painters, they know better than to claim that their current painting is finished when it is sitting there lifeless and unrealized. It is not easy to tell ourselves hard truths, but in the religion of creativity we prize that quality above all others.

> *So much of my life has been about self-effacement, pretense, masquerading, concealment, and indirection.*
>
> — MARLON RIGGS

There are several different aspects of truth-telling to examine in the next four weeks. This week we start with self-disclosure. If you get to know yourself (which means cracking your own defenses) and then you show yourself to others (which means going public and risking criticism) you have a shot at greatness. To consciously say "I am this person," to show your confusion, your secret fantasies, or your outrageous appetite to perfect strangers for the sake of truthfulness, are terrific accomplishments.

In this spirit, I was wondering how to show myself to you. It occurred to me to include an ordinary, unretouched photograph of me doing the dishes or typing at the keyboard. You'd see me and say, darn, I wish that guy were more heroic-looking, or cuter, or younger. And I'd have replied, "Too bad. Here I am. Take me or leave me." But I doubted that a photograph would show enough of me. So I thought, "How about a list?" Here it is.

ERIC MAISEL.

- Atheist.
- Not really a Maisel. (My mother married a Maisel, who died some years before I was born. Then she had a relationship with a Cohen, who'd changed his name to Cohane, to better his chances in the world of 1940s New York City politics. He claimed that he couldn't have children. He could.)
- Very careless. A slob. Though finicky, like Flaubert, about where the commas go.
- Sexual.
- Chubby since birth and probably before that.
- Skeptical.
- Not 5' 8", as I tend to say, but more like 5' 6", and shrinking.
- Cordial on the surface, but *this close* to writing off everyone.
- In love with the Constitution and the Bill of Rights.
- Faithful, primarily by staying home, where the main temptation is the refrigerator.
- Very grown up and very childish. Very courageous and very cowardly. Truthful and a liar. Modest and a show off.

That's a start.

You may do a kind of work—like computer programming, law, or medicine—where showing yourself seems beside the point. But a computer programmer stills needs to show himself to his loved ones, if he is to enjoy any intimacy. A doctor still needs to show herself to her patients, if she is to earn their trust. "Showing yourself" benefits you as a whole person, regardless of how it relates to your creative discipline.

EXERCISE 65 • *Show Yourself*

The first step is to reveal yourself in some way, on paper, through painting, in conversation, on your web page, by taking a stand, by making amends, in a letter, in a photograph, in a novel. Spend time today and tomorrow revealing who you are.

> *There's such incredible freedom just to say, "This is who I am, this is what I have. In all my strengths and weaknesses, this is who I am."*
>
> — JAMIE MCHUGH

Show yourself to me, if you like. My address is in the back of this book. You could send me the letter you wrote your mother, instead of sending it to her. You could send me a videotape of you eating or an audiotape of you singing. Notice your feelings when you drop your package in the mail. Maybe you'll feel nervous, embarrassed, pleased, or disappointed (because you're sure that I won't respond). This is what showing yourself feels like.

Or show yourself to someone else. Show yourself to your parents, your children, your old school friends, your audience, as risky as that feels. Chance exposing yourself. Chance looking ridiculous. Chance no one caring. The list of risks you'd be taking is very long and each risk on the list is a serious one. Do it anyway. It's the only way to assure your growth as an everyday creative person.

66. Reveal a Secret

It was in the second grade, I think. I'd been sick at the beginning of the school year and started classes several days late. The day I showed up, a girl who'd just moved into the neighborhood did so as well. The teacher had me go to the book closet and distribute the last two readers to both of us. One was new and the other was used. I kept the new one for myself.

One day when I was in about fourth or fifth grade, some kids were running races in the schoolyard. For no reason that I can identify, except that I am evil, during the last race I tripped the runner in the lane nearest me and sent him sprawling. No one saw me do it and I didn't volunteer a confession.

I wore my grandfather's only suit, which was too big for me in every possible way, to my first few seventh grade dances. I can't imagine how I looked and I don't want to picture it even now. Girls laughed, and by the end of seventh grade I stopped going to dances. This alone may explain why I've never owned a suit and why I associate suits with pain and misery.

I only occasionally did my homework in high school. More often I would copy my friend Lou's homework while we rode from Brooklyn to Manhattan on our daily trip to Stuyvesant High School. Lou would read the *New York Herald Tribune,* which he folded lengthwise down the middle like stockbrokers folded their *Wall Street Journals,* while I scribbled down his—meaningless to me—calculus and French grammar answers.

At Brooklyn College, I skipped almost all my classes and flunked out after about a year and a half.

It amuses me to this day that the only class I attended regularly was my Air Force ROTC class, because I loved marching. Not long after flunking out, as a so-to-speak logical next step, I enlisted in the army, during the height of the Vietnam war, because, apparently, I hadn't yet had my fill of marching.

> I made love to this girl without telling her that I was HIV positive, which was something incredible. For me, it's the only despicable thing I've done in my life.
>
> — CYRIL COLLARD

In the Army I shoplifted. I would come back from robbing the PX at some transit station, where my fellow soldiers and I were waiting to be shipped off to our Asian destinations, with some gaudy Hawaiian shirts hidden under my fatigues. I'd lay them out on my bunk and shout "Shirts!" to the GI's lounging around. Soldiers would drift on by, finger the cloth, and make their selection. I can think of many reasons why I did this—but here I just want to admit it.

In order to create, we need to feel comfortable revealing our secrets. Showing yourself is step one; telling your secrets is step two. Unless we possess that comfort level, we end up too concerned about protecting ourselves and can't make the connections that allow us to create. One of the reasons my adult students at St. Mary's College find the experience of writing an autobiography and five experiential learning essays transformative is that they are permitted and encouraged to tell important secrets about their own life. A woman will write for the first time about her abortion or her abusive marriage. A man will write for the first time about his alcoholic mother's emotional and physical abuse of him. These are not easy things to say out loud, either to ourselves or to another person. But my students discover that revealing secrets of this sort is both a healing experience and an opening to creativity.

Revealing our secrets to ourselves is an important act of liberation. Revealing them to others, in conversation with a mate or a friend or in our creative work, is another liberating act. When we reveal these secrets we grow more truthful. Then that truthfulness informs everything we do, whether it's writing technical articles or dealing with customers. If you say to yourself "I was humiliated as a child" or "I've done some wicked things," then reveal that secret to another person, you've greatly increased your chances of creating.

> *I have only to let myself go! So I have said all my life, yet I have never fully done it.*
>
> — HENRY JAMES

If we refuse to admit and confess the things that reflect poorly upon us or that make us look like monsters, we become habitually untruthful. The door to our creativity closes. Revealing secrets can bring us pain or get us into trouble, but worse pain and worse trouble await us if we keep silent.

EXERCISE 66 • *Reveal a Secret*

Reveal a secret. Take half an hour to write down some things that you don't want anyone to know about you. They could be about your fantasies, your irrational behaviors, the skeletons in your closet. Now decide how you're going to share these secrets: in a story, in an essay, in conversation with a friend, in a painting, or, if you need to start safely, in dialogue with yourself.

67. Serve Up a Sacred Cow

Most of us are phobic about blowing the whistle. We believe, with excellent justification, that people who point fingers tend to get those fingers lopped off. But refuting falsehoods is nevertheless a crucial part of an everyday creative person's makeup.

> An author's first duty is to let down his country.
> — BRENDAN BEHAN

If you turn off your truth-telling apparatus, so as to avoid making waves or getting into trouble, you'll also turn off your creativity. Shut down one and you'll shut down the other. Turn a blind eye to the insanity of the arms race and you can't write *Dr. Strangelove.* Turn a blind eye to the immorality of slavery and you can't write *Uncle Tom's Cabin.* Say "see no evil, hear no evil, do no evil" or "go along to get along" and you consign yourself to uncreativity. It is hard to tell the truth: it alienates the people you point your finger at and it's often dangerous. But blowing the whistle is an imperative of everyday creative people.

I dislike all religions, except the religion of creativity. I most passionately dislike religions touting a bearded man-God. I think that every religious leader who stands up and says "I know what God wants" is a flat-out liar. I think that bibles are written by mere mortals. I think that billions of people can all be wrong in believing in God. I think that believers haven't a clue, any more than I do, about the design of the universe. If I don't dare say these things to you, even as I risk alienating you, how can I demand that you serve up your own sacred cows? How can I ask you to be truthful if I mince my words or avoid hard subjects?

You may feel that I'm tying creativity to morality in an illegitimate way. If you narrowly define creativity as innovation, you'd be right. But remember how I'm using the word and what our religion is about. To create is to use your inner resources fully and completely, to use your heart,

> *Art has a prophetic role, denouncing the culture it lays bare.*
> — LANGDON GILKEY

mind, and hands in the service of meaningful work that makes you proud. Because I am adding that proviso—that the work should make you proud—I am naturally bringing morality into the picture. If you use your energy and ability to cleverly hide your company's polluting ways, to prove that poor people ought to remain poor, or to defend your claim that only your particular religious sect gets to heaven, you can still call yourself creative, since the word is as much yours as it is mine. But our meanings would be worlds apart.

As I use the word—maybe it should be creativity with a capital "C" (Creativity) or with an exclamation point (creativity!)—I am defining creativity as the intense and active search for truth, beauty, and goodness. In this paradigm, creators heroically strive to tell the truth about themselves and about their world. Serving up sacred cows—those commonly held, cherished beliefs that are neither true nor good—is a natural, if risky, part of a creator's journey.

EXERCISE 67 • *Pick a Lie, Blow the Whistle*

Today, list some of the important lies swirling around you. Maybe your school board is lying when it says that it's committed to creating excellent schools. Maybe the biggest charity in town is paying its executives obscenely large salaries and lying about how much of its proceeds are going to the needy. Maybe the federal government is lying when it says that its mandatory minimum drug sentencing policies aren't racist. Maybe the lies are closer to home: maybe broken cookies really do have calories and maybe your budget is leaking like a sieve not for mysterious reasons but because you're eating out four nights a week. Make a long list of the lies you know about or suspect.

Tomorrow, carefully examine your list of lies. Pick one that feels especially important to dispute. Then blow the whistle. Tell the truth as you understand it, as simply and directly as possible, maybe with a bumper sticker you purchase or have printed up: "The Constitution guarantees us freedom *from* religion." Write a letter to the editor or, if you feel ambitious, create a website devoted to your dissenting views. Do something direct, active, and fiery.

At the same time, invite a new creative project to percolate, one connected to the idea of serving up a sacred cow. Maybe you'll want to dispute conventional notions of conservatism in a well-reasoned nonfiction book you write. Maybe you'll want to start a cartoon strip that satirizes conspicuous consumption. Our theme for these four weeks is telling the truth: tell some.

WEEK 34

68. Balk

When I served in the army, I often balked. As a raw recruit during basic training, when our captain informed us that we'd have to pay for a new floor polisher out of our own pockets, I had to disagree. "Sir, I don't think that's right!" He dropped the idea. A year later, in Korea, when our just-arrived lieutenant expressed the desire to take our armored personnel carriers off-road and through some fields, I had to warn him: "Sir, the fields are mined!" We stayed on the road. When, a year after that, I listened to our company commander tell us that we'd have to attend the opening of the new Madison Square Garden in New York City, to assure Bob Hope of a large audience, I really couldn't agree. "Sir, I'm not sure we can be ordered to watch Bob Hope if we don't want to!" After an odd battle, with officers at the highest levels choosing sides, the trip to Madison Square Garden was made voluntary rather than mandatory.

> *When I am dead, let it be said of me: "He belonged to no school, to no church, to no institution, to no academy, least of all to any regime except the regime of liberty."*
>
> — GUSTAVE COURBET

How does this relate to creativity? In the following way. A fear of rebelling kills truthfulness and creativity. Creators need to be rebels even if they are also conservatives, because their goals are to save what deserves saving but also to change what needs changing. They need to be able to say "No, I won't!" and "You may have done it that way, but I need to do it this way!" Expressionist artists balked at the idea that representing objects was the only way to paint; Copernicus balked at the idea that the sun revolved around the earth; e. e. cummings balked at the idea of capitalization; Clara Schumann balked at the idea that only men could compose; Martin Scorsese balked at the idea that a film portraying Christ with weaknesses would be too controversial make. In order to create and to live one's truth, an everyday creative person must balk regularly.

Of course, it isn't possible to balk every single time you encounter something you find offensive or untruthful. There are unfortunate compromises that each of us must make to pay the bills and to get along in society. Think of Goya. He indicted human savagery in his paintings of executions and massacres. But he also painted commissioned portraits of nobility and the wealthy. You too will probably make compromises of this sort. On some days you'll take photo portraits of clients because your family needs new shoes. On other days you'll balk at the conspiracy of silence about America's starving children and aim your camera in their direction. This is far from an ideal solution; but even though you can't balk at everything, you can still balk magnificently.

> *They don't ask much of you. They only want you to hate the things you love and to love the things you despise.*
> — BORIS PASTERNAK, ON SOVIET BUREAUCRATS

What if you're fascinated by your current creative work but fear its consequences? Can you balk even there, when you love what you're doing? Take the—perhaps apocryphal—story told about the inventor Nikola Tesla. Tesla supposedly invented the first laser, demonstrated it to reporters, and then destroyed his new invention, explaining that he feared man would only use it for warfare. But even in this exceptional case of balking, Tesla could not prevent himself from creating his laser and flaunting it at least once before destroying it—thereby allowing other scientists to get wind of it.

This story should remind us just how hard it is to balk—when an idea fascinates us, when we're looking for fame and glory, when there's money to be made, in any of countless situations. Isn't it equally hard for a writer not to write a book that he knows will sell but that he finds unworthy and for a biologist not to pursue a problem whose solution will amount to a scientific breakthrough but also a societal ill? Isn't it equally hard for a painter to stop producing his trademark paintings, which are in demand and fetch a handsome price, and for a businessperson not to use his creative energies to find ruthless ways to eliminate the competition? Balking *is* hard—and eternally necessary.

EXERCISE **68** • *Think About Balking*

During the next few days, you're likely to encounter some situation where you feel it would be wise or ethical of you to balk. Maybe a design commission will materialize that pays handsomely but robs you of too much painting time. Maybe a singing job will come up but the musical director says that he can't pay you—there's only enough money to pay the instrumentalists. When such a situation arises, consider balking. If you do balk, congratulate yourself, no matter what consequences flow from your decision. If you can't balk, make a pledge with yourself to be braver next time.

WEEK 35

69. Make Difficulties

Everyday creative people, in order to be true to themselves, have no choice but to make difficulties. They need to launch ambitious creative projects, object to the prevailing theory in their field if they disagree with it, expose themselves to ridicule by admitting some hard truth in their film or novel. This is their job.

Of course, on one level it would be easier not to do these difficult things. No one is demanding that we do them. Our children would just as soon we didn't reveal unflattering secrets about our home life or make a spectacle of ourselves with our performance art. Our parents would just as soon we didn't blow the whistle at work and risk our job. Our literary agent doesn't want to be given our most challenging nonfiction book to handle, the one that she'll find virtually impossible to sell. Our gallery representative doesn't want our antireligious paintings, even if he himself is a secularist. No one is demanding that we make these difficulties.

When all combine in every way to make everything easier, people will want difficulty. I conceived it as my task to make difficulties everywhere.

— SOREN KIERKEGAARD

But we really have no choice. Think of Mozart. In his own time, Mozart was castigated for composing music that was far too difficult. Musicians found his pieces too hard to play, and listeners complained that his music required too much attention and interrupted conversation. Only in a few places—in Prague, for instance—was Mozart's music accepted and applauded. But surely he had no choice but to compose exactly as his heart dictated. Was Mozart to write elevator music or *Don Giovanni?*

Of course when you make necessary difficulties, consequences will follow. You'll write a quiet, complex screenplay and the Hollywood executive with whom you meet will edify you: "Maybe I'll finance your movie, if you take out the slow parts and change your hero's age from forty to thirteen. What *were* you thinking?" You'll cram your novel full of a dozen characters, because you wanted to make a huge tapestry, and discover that you've created a mob scene instead. You'll object to a theory in your field and discover that your peers consider you a traitor and that your grant money is mysteriously drying up. These are the sorts of consequences for which we must ready ourselves.

An income and a good night's sleep are already hard enough to come by. Life is a difficult enough affair, so why pile difficulty upon difficulty? Because the best things are also the most difficult things. Acting justly is always a difficulty, but still it's our best course. Living with another person leads to a few difficulties, but still we should opt for love. Creating deeply is a difficulty of the first magnitude—and our only possible choice is to cast our vote for it.

> *If you want me to play only the notes without any specific color dynamics, I will never make one mistake.*
> — VLADIMIR HOROWITZ

EXERCISE 69 • *Make Difficulties*

For two of the next three days, invent some real difficulties for yourself.

Today, imagine expanding your business, learning a tricky painting technique, adding a virtuoso concerto to your violin repertoire, or attempting some other project that strikes you as really difficult.

Tomorrow, up the ante. Think about expanding your business not just in-state but also out-of-state. Begin a large painting employing the technique you just started learning. Select a second concerto to master. Whether you actually do this exercise or only picture it in your mind's eye, try to get a sense of what it feels like to pose yourself—and then meet—some real difficulties.

The day after tomorrow, relax. Make a cup of hot chocolate. Put in some miniature marshmallows. Difficulty isn't everything. Breathe easy. Do nothing, if you like. Watch a movie. Of course, you may find that staying calm is its own difficulty now, so immersed have you become in your mighty project. Relax, if you can. Or rush back to the profound difficulties of your current work.

70. Explain Yourself

Often we're in the dark about our current creative project even though we're deeply immersed in it. We may have little idea where we're going or what we're intending to say. Forcing yourself to explain what you're up to can be a big help in such circumstances. It can benefit you tremendously to explain to yourself (or to another person) what your current creative project is about: what you intend it to say, what difficulties you're encountering, how it fits into your overall body of work, and so on. Too often we're unaware of the significant pitfalls facing us until we make an effort at explanation.

You might argue that there are better reasons *not* to explain what you're attempting to do in your current work. Trying to explain your work might interrupt or even derail the creative process, for example. Since so much of the creative process is about "not knowing," you might think that forcing out a description of your current project while it's still metamorphosing could do it real harm. You may also feel that an explanation of your work is too pale an imitation of the work itself and never does it any justice.

The paraphrase of a novel can sound shallow and even ridiculous; talking thematically about painting, music, or dance can feel like an even greater folly. Finally, you may fear that your ideas will be stolen if you share them with another person.

These are all legitimate concerns. There are enough stories about the theft of ideas in science, the arts, and business, for example, to suggest that you aren't just being paranoid. But often the value of explaining yourself—to another person or at least to yourself—outweighs any negative consequences. Your honorable attempt at explanation, where you try to convey the essence of your work and its relation to other work in your field and your tradition, can help you see its strengths and weaknesses for the first time. Suddenly you see what it needs and whether it's on the right track or a wrong one.

> *Three years ago I was only doing large abstract work, very impersonal and influenced by landscape. Now I'm letting the subject matter of AIDS and the Black Death and illness reside in me more, with more availability.*
> — ROBERT FARBER

A new client, a well-known documentary filmmaker, recently came to see me in a quandary. She was about to launch into a film about peasant life in Ecuador. But something about her choice of subject bothered her. I asked her to explain herself. Why had she chosen this particular topic? How did it relate to her previous work? What theme did she feel she'd be pursuing? What had the initial impetus been? Although she'd described her project previously to scores of people in order to get funding for the film, it soon became clear that she'd never really explained it to herself.

Now, as she made that effort, haltingly at first and then more fluently, she began to see what was bothering her. She'd thought that the film was about preserving a record of "the old ways" of Ecuadorian peasants. The idea had arisen out of feelings of nostalgia—but not, she began to see, a nostalgia for the old ways of Ecuador, to which she had no real connection. Rather, she was nostalgic for her own childhood and grieving for her recently deceased parents. It turned out that instead of making a film about Ecuador she needed to make a film about her own family.

> *If I, a living witness, one who experienced those times, don't speak about them, then others who did not experience or witness those times will invent their own version of them.*
>
> — ANATOLY RYBAKOV

How do you go about explaining your current work? As clearly and directly as possible. "A mad obsessiveness and competitiveness are built into the American way of life and I think I can communicate something about that in a tale about a ship captain and a whale." "There are two competing urges in the American psyche, to be left alone and to do the right thing, and I think I can capture that inner conflict in a story about a nightclub owner in Casablanca during World War II." Your goal is to get to the nub of your idea in so clear a way that you feel confident about what you're doing.

There's no room in the work itself for such explanations. You can't, if you are Monet, explain in small print among the water lilies what you mean to do as an artist. The work must speak for itself. But you have the power, and often very good reasons, to explain the work to yourself and to others. This requires some practice, but when you become accomplished at explaining yourself, you can do a better job of interesting others in your work and of maintaining your own interest.

EXERCISE **70** • *Explain Yourself*

Start an E-mail dialogue with a friend in which you tell her about your current work, invite questions, and endeavor to answer those questions. Ask your friend to be diligent and even tough; if she feels you're being vague, evasive, muddled, or untruthful in your explanations, she should continue grilling you until you've honestly and completely explained yourself.

WEEK 36

71. Aim for Truthfulness

Everyday creative people stand up for the truth, love the truth, and even risk their lives for the truth. But the truth is often hard to discern. Take, for example, America's dropping two atomic bombs on Japan. Were those necessary or unnecessary acts? How would you arrive at the truth of the matter? Indeed, what "truth" would you be looking for?

I think these questions are very difficult to answer. If you ask instead whether those bombings took a horrendous toll, both in the moment and for generations of Japanese to follow, the answer is simple. But if you ask whether Imperial Japan would have sur-

> *A lie hides the truth.*
> *A story tries to find it.*
> — PAULA FOX

rendered if we'd merely demonstrated the power of atomic weapons without using them on populated areas, the answer appears harder to come by. Some people argue that immediate surrender would have followed if we'd ignited an atomic weapon over Tokyo Bay for all to see. Others are positive that the

Japanese military wouldn't have been swayed by even that awesome display. Who can be sure?

But why didn't we drop an atomic bomb over Tokyo Bay and see how Japan reacted? Wasn't that the reasonable course? Possibly. But with the benefit of hindsight, there are even more complications to consider. It seems entirely possible that unless huge numbers of people were sacrificed at Hiroshima and Nagasaki, the human race would never have understood the full horror of atomic weapons. Then our eventual nuclear destruction might even have been guaranteed—perhaps during the Cuban missile crisis.

> *Life must be loved or it is lost, but it should never be loved too well. Keep your hatred of a lie, and keep your power of indignation.*
>
> — LETTER TO HIS UNBORN CHILD, FROM AN EXECUTED PARTISAN

If the human race was perhaps saved from nuclear annihilation because we dropped those two atomic bombs, then you'd have to say that they were necessary acts—even compulsory ones. If you agree with this analysis, then dropping the second bomb taught the world an ever bigger lesson about human nature than only dropping the first, because, with even less military justification for its use, it spoke volumes about how casually human beings could deploy weapons of mass destruction.

Truthfulness is at the heart of the creative enterprise. But if you can't know the truth, you can at least refuse to accept too-simple answers and vehemently disagree with what you know to be false. You may not know if homosexuality is a choice, a product of environment, the result of psychological issues, or a biological predisposition. But you certainly know that at this moment in our learning curve nobody else knows either. If someone stands up and says, "Gays are sinners for choosing homosexuality," you are right to leap up and cry, "You simply don't know that!" An everyday creative person may not know the truth of a given matter—and often she doesn't—but she can still demand of herself that she be as truthful as possible.

EXERCISE 71 • *Aim for Truthfulness*

Think of a question with many sides to it, like:

- Should it be legal to use marijuana?
- Should trade with China be pursued or should China's human rights' violations be condemned?
- Should babies of one race be raised by adoptive parents of a different race?
- Should Nazis be allowed to demonstrate in Jewish and African-American communities?
- Should a president strive to be moral or strive to be effective?
- To what extent should a woman and a man both have a say about whether to abort their fetus?

Pick one such question to examine. Study it from as many angles as you can. Spend a few days writing down your thoughts and observations. Your goal isn't to come to a final conclusion but to practice handling complexity and to learn how to aim yourself in the direction of truthfulness.

72. Live Your Truth

One of my clients made a decision two decades ago, in his midtwenties, to give up his dream of becoming a writer. Instead, he entered his father's highly successful import/export business. He regretted that decision and had for years tried to return to the writing life by penning stage plays that, unfortunately, he didn't like very much. Now, he told me, he wanted to start an ambitious novel, part adventure yarn and part family study, set in Placerville, California, during the Gold Rush days. The hero would be a young man trying to get out from under the thumb of his tyrannical father and finally succeeding.

I could tell, as I listened to my client explain his doubts about the book, that he was struggling with the question of how much of the autobiographical relationship between his father and himself to allow into the novel. It seemed that, on balance, he'd decided not to show himself, not to reveal any secrets, not, in short, to address what was on his mind. I brought this up and wondered if he wasn't setting himself up for unnecessary difficulties by designing a novel that called for a real exploration of a father/son relationship but that avoided revealing the author's own true thoughts and feelings.

I suggested that he either write the adventure yarn or commit to exploring his past—one or the other. The next time we met he explained that he'd changed his mind entirely. He didn't want to write about his family and he didn't want to set a novel in the past. Now he wanted to write a novel based on an interesting news clipping he'd just come across, about a loophole in the US immigration laws around which a political thriller could be fashioned. I agreed that it sounded as if he had a clever idea for a novel. But I wondered if part of his dissatisfaction with his stage plays, a dissatisfaction that still rankled, didn't stem from the way he'd tackled "interesting ideas" in them, too—rather than genuine feelings.

> *Modern man has lost the option of silence.*
> — WILLIAM S. BURROUGHS

The next week he announced that he'd abandoned his latest idea. Now he wanted to write an honest book about fathers and sons. But he intended for his main character, the father, to be a mild-mannered gentleman. Why, I asked, wasn't the father a tyrannical monster like his own father, since transforming him into a milk toast would do so much damage to the novel's dramatic energy? At first he replied that he wanted to radically fictionalize the main character, so that his novel remained a novel and didn't veer toward a memoir. Then he admitted that he wanted to make the villain a mere ghost of a villain, so as not to conjure up his own feelings of rage against his father. By the end of that session he agreed that the father in the novel would have to be large, volcanic, cruel . . . in short, real.

Our work is ongoing. My client is approaching telling his truth. He is also approaching living it, as he struggles to find ways to deal with his feelings about his father and ways to make their still-volatile relationship less acrimonious. Living our truth is not an easy thing for any of us to do. Darwin withheld his thoughts about evolution for years, because he feared its devastating effects on theology. I know of actors who have stopped auditioning after a critical review of one performance, even though they wanted to keep acting. Scientists have worked on research projects with no redeeming social value, because the grant money was there. Writers have followed a good book with a mediocre sequel be-

> *I was always very, very diplomatic. I never had any enemies. Now I have tons of them and I don't care.*
>
> — EDMUND WHITE

cause they could muster enthusiasm for the size of the book advance offered, if not for its subject matter. We are all weak and fallible some of the time.

Living your truth means facing your demons, creating deeply, resolving your inner conflicts, minimizing your weaknesses, and doing the other work I'm describing in this book. If you'd like to paint but aren't painting, live your truth by starting. If you'd like to teach but teaching scares you, live your truth by starting. Take a giant—or a small—step in the direction of living your truth.

EXERCISE **72** • *Live Your Truth*

Here at the end of your month of work on truthfulness, I'd like you to spend some time writing down your truth and how you'd like to live it. Write down your answers to the following questions:

- What are my guiding principles?
- What are my deepest desires?
- What are my shortcomings?
- What sort of life do I want to lead?
- How can I get there?
- What's the most truthful creative work in my power to do?

PART 10

Be Love

Weeks 37-40

73. Renew Your Vows

Do you remember how songs gladdened your heart when you were growing up? Did you also love magic shows and protozoa wriggling under the lens of your microscope? Dance class and romantic movies? I bet you did. I bet you were secretly married to writing or singing or the study of biology. Maybe you even wrote your vows down in your diary: to faithfully paint or write or break the genetic code one day. Do you remember those vows?

> *For this vocation of writing I was and am willing to die, and I consider very few other things of the slightest importance.*
>
> — KATHERINE ANNE PORTER

Then you grew up. You had to think about making money and fulfilling the other needs of everyday life. You got buffeted this way and that. Maybe relationships broke up, maybe you drank too much, maybe you waitressed for too many years. These and other hard realities took their toll. One toll they may have taken is on your heart. You may have stopped loving what you loved as a child because the demands of living tired you out. If that happened, it's hurt your chances of creating.

Creativity is a religion rooted in love—a love of song, a love of protozoa, a love of magic, a love of movies, a love of what human beings can create, a love of life. We need to love in order to feel motivated to create. It would be excellent if you could let that love from childhood return right now. Love your creative nature again. Love your current and future creative efforts. Love what creativity has to offer you. Love practicing this religion of ours. Love the truth, beauty, and goodness inside of you. Was there ever a better time to invite that love to return?

EXERCISE 73 • *Renew Your Vows*

Tomorrow you'll be going to a wedding: yours. So plan to take tomorrow off, or else save this exercise for the weekend.

Let's say that you're a painter. Tomorrow you and your painting life will get married. If at some time in the past you consciously took a vow to love and honor your painting life, then tomorrow you'll be taking your vows for the second time. But more likely this will be the first time you ceremonially pledged to love and honor your painting life. (If you're a chemist, marry chemistry. If you're a ceramicist, marry ceramics. If you're a singer, marry song.)

You're not marrying any particular painting but the imago of painting. An imago is an idealized image of a person, often a parent. It's an odd word with a nice ring to it and we'll use it to suit our purposes by redefining it as the very essence of an art. Can you picture your painting imago? Is it a stretched, primed canvas? Is it a great painting from the past—all dark, from the seventeenth century, or all bright, from the twentieth? Is it a painting you yourself painted? Think for a while and settle on your painting imago.

You'll also need vows. How about the simple, "I take you, painting imago, and I hope you take me"? Or some lines from a favorite poem? Or vows from a wedding you attended and loved? Or inspiring words from a tradition you respect? Or a passage from a novel? Or vows that you write? Wherever the words come from, the pledge should run deep. What you're communicating—to yourself, of course—is that creativity, whatever else it is, is also a commitment that lasts a lifetime, through thick and thin.

> *When there is a great love there are always miracles.*
> — WILLA CATHER

Select your wedding music. Get dressed nicely. Put the music on. Take your painting imago by the hand. (You will only look silly walking down the aisle all alone if you think that looks silly.) Get emotional; get anxious; feel like you're getting married. An oleander bush in your garden can be your minister. Daisies can be the guests. Pine trees can be the pilasters holding up the vault of your cathedral. Step outside into the sunshine.

Maybe you've put a runner down. March slowly, following the tempo of the music. Arrive at the altar made by a pair of gnarled rose bushes. Acknowledge the oleander minister. Say your vows—each of you, in turn, with feeling. (You could also do this with actual guests, an actual minister, and actual catering. That would be splendid, but a much bigger undertaking.)

Pronounce youself person and painting.

Love your art. Does all this talk about loving art seem foolish? Just think back to when you were eleven, to the books you loved and the way you stayed up reading far into the night. That was about love, my friend; our religion is rooted in love.

74. Love Logic and Intuition

The shortest definition of creativity is "having ideas." You're creative when you generate ideas. Sometimes it feels as if there are two ways to generate ideas, a "left brain" logical way and a "right brain" intuitive way. I personally doubt whether this distinction

> *The sunflower's secret is one of hidden geometry.*
> — ESTHER WARNER DENDEL

represents two different coins or even two sides of the same coin. I think logic and intuition are the same thing. When we're logical we're aware that we're making connections. When we're intuitive we're just less aware of the process: the connections arrive full-blown.

In both cases the end results are well-made connections. When you create, you get to be your most logical self and also your most intuitive self. You get to know how things combine—color with color, sound with sound, word with word, idea with idea—in ways that would make an alchemist green with envy.

Sometimes you'll be very aware of your process and able to hear yourself saying internally, "If I do this, then that would happen, at which point I could follow up with *that,* and then *that* would happen." This is how logic sounds. The great chess player Akiba Rubinstein, when he wanted to praise one of his games, would say, "I played logically." To an observer it looked as if irrational things were happening—insane sacrifices, unconventional gambits, mysterious moves whose meaning they couldn't fathom. But Rubinstein was simply calculating. Any computer advanced enough to play with him—fast-enough computers with artful-enough programs beat grandmasters today—would have nodded.

Logic is simply "making sense." We are built to love it when things make sense. Both great science and great art are logical. If you draw a character and invite us to inhabit her, but then, to shore up a plot problem, force her to act against her own inner logic, we know it. We get irritated, maybe even furious. If the solution to your mystery is illogical, if the objects in your painting are out of alignment, if the ideas in your theory don't add up, we get upset and edgy. We don't like what you've done, because we're built for logic, we love it, and we need it.

> *Your ears will always lead you right, but you must know why.*
> — ANTON VON WEBERN

We are also built for intuition and to love intuition. Creative people trust intuition and cultivate it because it is another way the mind has of making right connections. You visit the oak tree in your backyard and begin to paint without any conscious sense of "If I do this, then that will happen." You aren't aware of your own logical processes but they're proceeding nonetheless. The connections get made and, out of an intuitive understanding of what you're aiming for, you create a recognizable oak or a pure rectangle, one that's brown and green or as blue and red as a Fauvist fantasy, one that connotes sturdiness or that undulates so sinuously that it looks ready to mate.

Van Gogh once realized that he was using up all of his paints at the same rate, even though he'd ordered them in varying quantities—say, three blues for every two yellows for every one red. He wrote to his brother, Theo, that this had to mean that although he had no conscious conception of what he was about to paint, he must have some intuitive plan for each series of paintings. How else would he know the precise quantity of paints to order?

We love this intuitive ability of ours. For instance, I conceived this book as having eighty-eight sections, intuitively analogizing its shape to a piano keyboard and each section to a different note. But along the line that plan was changed and a different number of sections was mapped out. Yet, in the course of actually writing the book, I discovered one day that, excluding the introduction and conclusion, I had returned to exactly eighty-eight sections. We love it that we can intuit in these ways. We love these two profiles of the same face, that we are logical and intuitive both.

EXERCISE 7 4 • *Articulate Your Love of Logic and Intuition*

Sometimes a person feels biased toward logic or toward intuition, as if they were opposed or contradictory processes that one had to choose between. But they aren't. Embrace them both. To help yourself do that, spend a little time, at least half an hour on each, completing the following two prompts:

"I love logic because . . ."
"I love intuition because . . ."

Don't choose between logic and intuition. Love them both.

75. Locate Your Better Nature

James Dickey was an excellent writer. But he was also an alcoholic and a liar. His son remembers being regaled by the story of Dickey losing his first wife when she contracted blood poisoning, had to have her arm amputated, and subsequently died. Decades later Dickey confessed that none of that was true. Why did he tell his son that tall tale? What earthly reason did he have for telling that lie? To see his little boy's eyes open wide?

> My children are elephants—they take up so much room. Paulo is the most disgusting son in the world.
> — PABLO PICASSO

Well, I like to be interesting, too. I like to lie, too. Sometimes I feel the need to lie just because, with so many sanctimonious lies posing as truths swirling about, if I were to tell the truth I'd feel like a patsy. Even though I am aware of this shadow side in me, sometimes I fall short and unleash it. We have to be careful, you and I, about that shadow side—careful not to unleash the darkness inside each of us. We must be careful not to be too self-centered, too demanding, too cruel, too rude, too cavalier in the way we treat others. As with any religion, the religion of creativity asks of its members that they be righteous.

The religion of creativity is not just about people innovating. In our religion, we withhold the label of creative if someone isn't a good person as well as an artful one. At the very least, we qualify our praise. We say about a terrific composer who's also a bastard, "His creativity is restricted to his composing. He's not creative at life, because he hasn't mastered truth, beauty, *and* goodness." No dictionary definition of creativity includes ethics as an element, but in our religion we do, by reminding ourselves that the creative work and its creator should both be exemplary.

> *I would gladly have thrown my wife and children in, if that was necessary to keep the kiln fire going.*
>
> — PABLO PICASSO

There is necessary arrogance in a creative person's nature, the arrogance of a living creature demanding to fulfill its destiny. But another sort of arrogance can also arise, the arrogance of a best-selling writer who looks down on midlist writers or a choreographer who feels entitled to curse and belittle his dancers. There is necessary narcissism in a creative person's nature, a healthy narcissism that is the self's righteous love of self. But an ugly narcissism can also be bred, one that strangles the artist's own humanity. Who was more creative than Picasso or more revered as an artist? But he was also a cruel man, insulting to his own children. Should he be forgiven his cruelty because he could paint? No. No creative person is justified in being cruel because he is creative—creative in the limited sense of painting or writing well.

If the religion of creativity were just narrowly about talent or innovation, we wouldn't bother ourselves thinking about the whole person. We'd picture an artist standing raptly in front of his easel and consider that the whole picture. But if creativity is a religion to live by, it should include the whole person, a whole person striving to be ethical as well as innovative.

EXERCISE **75** • *Be a Good Person*

For forty-eight hours, practice being a good person. No, let's go further. Spend the next forty-eight hours being saintly.

You laugh. But why not be a saint? Are these some of your objections?

- People will trample you.
- You'll get hoodwinked.
- People aren't worth it.
- There's no time for goodness.
- You don't have the energy.
- It's survival of the fittest out there.
- What is goodness, anyway?
- You can't see the payoff.
- The good deeds you can imagine doing seem trivial.
- You'd rather be bad than good.
- You suspect you don't have what it takes to be good.

Some of your objections may be valid. Even if they weren't, sainthood isn't easy. But try. Try each of the following at least once during the next few days:

- Praise someone, especially another artist.
- Do an anonymous good deed.
- Make a small measure of amends to someone you've harmed.
- Spend time with someone you usually short-change on time.

Maybe you'll heal some old wounds as you reach out lovingly. Maybe you'll release some envy or anger that's not really serving you. Give it a try. There's plenty of time to be a genius. For a little while, try goodness.

76. Help Friends and Strangers

This morning a friend will call to confer on the book she's currently writing, about thriving after your children leave home. A fiction writer and executive director of an environmental nonprofit corporation, she is tackling nonfiction for the first time. We've been friends for twenty-five years and nothing could feel better than having this opportunity to help her. With other friends, I've offered to call up editors I know to pitch book ideas, facilitated writing workshops and been paid in house plants, gotten them ghostwriting jobs, entered into E-mail dialogue in support of their current projects. These are among the good deeds possible in the religion of creativity, where fostering creativity in ourselves and in others ultimately benefits us all.

Sometimes my help is turned down. An unpublished friend of mine who's working on a book about relationships said that she preferred that I not contact a likely editor. I asked her why, not because I felt insulted or rejected but because I wanted to know what was on her mind. If she was afraid that her book might be accepted—"fear of success" looks to be a real phenomenon—I wanted to have the chance to discuss that fear with her. She replied that she couldn't say what was on her mind exactly, but she had a plan for marketing her book that didn't include me. With a client who is paying me not to take such answers at face value, I might have persisted. With my friend, I didn't. I still wanted to help, but I took no for an answer.

Many well-known creators have succeeded because a friend championed their work. Dostoyevsky's roommate read his first novel and took it by hand to Russia's leading literary critic, who loved it, praised it, and caused it to be published. Faulkner got his foot in the door when a published friend of his complained, "If you don't make me read your whole novel, I'll see to it that it gets published!" Directors hire their actor children, writers collaborate with their mates, soloists premiere the compositions of former school buddies. This is as it should be. The people who know us should help us, if we are worthy, and we should help the worthy people we know.

> *Barney [Barnett Newman] was one of those encouraging people; for a young artist to meet a real artist—just knowing him—made you realize that you were an artist.*
>
> — LARRY POONS

I think it is loving and righteous to offer help to our friends, even if they then reject that help and turn us down. Strangers, too, deserve our help. I regularly talk to strangers who know my work and call to discuss their problems. I don't see these phone calls as impositions, nor do I see these callers as potential clients. I see them as everyday creative people like myself who are struggling with their work, their blocks, their relationships, the marketplace, and all the rest. I know that if I got too many of these calls— or too many unpleasant calls—I'd have to adjust my thinking about my accessibility. But for now I can chat with strangers and try to be of as much help as possible.

Strangers also send me manuscripts, which they hope I will endorse. I'm glad to receive them, not only because they keep me informed about the creativity literature but because each book represents a human success story. I try to read these manuscripts and endorse them if I can. Again, if I received hundreds of unsolicited manuscripts, as agents and editors do, my good humor might dissolve and my desire to be of help vanish. But since I receive only the occasional one, I can be generous.

Diego [Rivera] and Frida [Kahlo] had an open house. In that house you'd see a king and you'd see a laborer. He never made a distinction—never. There was nothing he wouldn't give you.
— LOUISE NEVELSON

If you are in a position to help, please do. That will guarantee you entrance into Creativity Heaven. If you need help, ask for it. You will want to be careful about how you ask, reminding yourself that people are busy and maybe even overwhelmed in their own lives. Ask carefully, but *do* ask—clearly, directly, and without embarrassment. If you want to study with a certain well-known artist, approach him. You may doubt that he takes on students, but what harm can there be in asking? If you want to bounce your ideas about the politics of race off the preeminent writer in your field, write her. Maybe her secretary will write back to say that she's too busy to respond. But maybe the voice you hear on the phone one day will be hers.

EXERCISE **76** • *Help a Friend; and Ask a Friend for Help*

Think of a friend who could use help with his or her creative life. Does your friend Mary, who's stopped writing, need encouragement? Could your friend Bill use your support as his art buddy? Can you take time away from your own efforts to look at your friend Martha's photographs? If there's a way you could be of use, make an offer.

Do you yourself need help? Which friend or stranger might provide it? Think the matter through, prepare yourself, and then ask for what you need.

77. Love Another Person

It isn't enough to create. In our religion, it's also important to love at least one other person—that's the minimum, not the maximum!—in addition to the novels, songs, or scientific theories we create and love. Happiness and mental health flow from this well-rounded way of being and our chances of deeply creating are improved when we're bolstered by love.

I hope that the advice I'm giving you is unnecessary and that you are already in a loving relationship. But it may be that you haven't found the right person to love yet; or it may be that your own temperament, failings, habits, and goals are preventing you from loving. Possibly it's a little of both. If you aren't in a loving relationship with another human being, I hope you'll think about why that might be the case and what in your nature might be contributing to that absence.

Are you perhaps too self-centered? Too embittered? Too critical? Too impatient? Have you got it into your head that living with another person creates more problems than blessings? Think this through. You may learn what George Bernard Shaw discovered about himself: "I was taught when I was young that if people would only love one another, all would be well with the world. I found when I tried to put that into practice, not only were other people seldom lovable but I wasn't very lovable myself."

What are the contours of a good intimate relationship? Every successful intimate relationship rests on the following twenty building blocks. Both partners commit to:

The sonata grew out of my feelings for my husband as well as from my particular fondness for the violin. I loved Joseph's sense of timing, the way he could shape a melodic line, and I loved the kind of sonorities you could get out of this wonderful instrument.

— ELLEN TAAFFE ZWILICH

1. The care of each other's solitude
2. The maintenance of emotional security
3. The maintenance of meaning
4. The maintenance of passion
5. The creation of at least occasional happiness
6. A gentle demanding of discipline from oneself and one's partner
7. A gentle exchanging of truths
8. An acceptance of the limits of the human
9. A minimizing of one's own unwanted qualities
10. The support of each other's career and creative life
11. The maintenance of friendship
12. A monitoring of moods in oneself and one's partner
13. An acceptance of difficulties
14. A commitment to one's role as ethical witness
15. The management of one's own self, life, and journey
16. Careful communicating
17. A bringing of one's creativity to the partnership
18. The maintenance of a present and a future orientation

19. Fair treatment of oneself and one's partner
20. The creation of a safe environment

The relationship goal of an everyday creative person is fashioning an ever-evolving partnership with a loved one, where each partner respects the other's creative efforts and has his or her own creative efforts respected in return. This fine relating eludes many everyday creative people—indeed, eludes many human beings—but it remains the prize upon which we want to keep our eye.

> *To love another person you have to undertake some fragment of their destiny.*
> — QUENTIN CRISP

EXERCISE 77 • *Love Another Person*

If you're currently in a loving relationship with another person, take the opportunity over the next few days to say "I love you" and to engage in some acts of love and friendship. Do your lover a special favor. Work harder to break that habit of yours that drives him or her crazy. Open your heart even more than usual. Let your lover know how lucky you feel to have him or her in your life.

If you aren't currently in a loving relationship, try to engage in the self-analysis I suggested earlier. Make an attempt to learn what in your own nature, if anything, is preventing you from loving and being loved. If you can identify something—say, that you hold your creative work as more important than your relationships—think through whether this makes sense to you. If you do identify features of your personality that you'd like to change, map out a clear plan for changing them. Reaffirm the value of intimacy and your dream for a loving relationship.

78. Be Sexual

If you bring your sexual impulses to your creative work—if you come to the geological problem you're trying to solve aroused, if you fantasize about wild sex with a stranger while playing a repressed wife on stage, if sexual acts are on your mind as you write your book about supply-side economics—you'll be working from deep in the genetic code, down where life wants to make new life and feel good in the process. Creativity and sexuality have a lot in common—among them desire, arousal, and climax—and feeling sexy can give your work an energy and sheen that nothing else can.

> *I always start writing with a clean piece of paper and a dirty mind.*
> — PATRICK DENNIS

Many creators have likened their creative efforts to making love. Janis Joplin said that of her singing, Arthur Rubinstein of his piano playing, Isaac Bashevis Singer of his short-story writing, Leonard Bernstein of his conducting. You wouldn't think that I'd have a hard time convincing you to bring your sexual impulses to your creative efforts, so natural are the connections between the two. But I bet you haven't been offered this advice too often before. Were creativity and sexuality encouraged in the same breath in elementary school? In middle school? In high school? In college? I doubt it. Creativity and sexuality are not typically presented as ideas that ought to be linked.

How might you go about marrying them? Let's say that you're a mathematician and you've been examining a set theory problem whose solution has eluded you so far. Probably, as you go about your work engaging in mind experiments and testing hypotheses, you conjure up equations and not trysts, mathematical formulae and not escapades in Crete or Lesbos. But since your problem has proven intractable, you might want to try a new tack by injecting a little sexuality into the process. You might picture the potential audience for your solution—other mathematicians—naked. Wouldn't that awaken some ideas that have been lying dormant? Wouldn't more neurons enlist themselves in the hunt for a solution with a scent of sex in the air?

> The domain of rhythm extends from the spiritual to the carnal.
>
> — BRUNO WALTER

Maybe you've been laboring on a novel for a long time now. There are many reasons why your novel might not be working: maybe you don't know what it's about yet and are putting off wrestling with that question, maybe you got too engrossed in atmospherics, maybe your plot is hackneyed but you don't want to admit that. The list of possible problems is a long one. But one reason might be that you don't know your characters well enough. If you keep them vague and distant, you won't feel motivated to write about them. So get to know them better by imagining their sex lives.

Be a voyeur. Picture each of your characters. To whom are they attracted? In what circumstances do they catch fire? Do they rip off their clothes or always undress carefully? What was their most embarrassing sexual moment? Their most painful? Their most ecstatic? Write down a few details about each character that speak volumes about his or her nature. I'd be surprised if this exercise didn't provoke you to resume your novel—and didn't improve it dramatically.

EXERCISE **78** • *Create Sexually*

You will need a lover for this exercise. Of course, having a lover isn't a bad idea in its own right.

After dinner, tell your lover that you would like to set up a date to make love that night, if he or she is interested. If your lover agrees, thank him or her and go directly to your work space. Start a new project, one you pick just for the sake of this exercise—some new painting, short story, or song. A frankly sexual one might be the most appropriate choice, but any will do. As you work on your new sculpture or poem, allow yourself to visualize you and your lover making love. This will be an odd dual concentration, but you'll get the hang of it. Get all of your senses involved. Get, as the phrase has it, "into it."

Have a glass of ice water handy. If you get too aroused, douse yourself with some of the ice water. Keep working; but keep returning to your sexual feelings too. Stop before it gets too late—remember, your lover is waiting!—and assess how the creating went. If the work turned out poorly, laugh it off and go make love. If the work turned out well, store this exercise away in your memory. You'll have added a new way of working to your repertoire. Now you get to make love. Hasn't this been a good evening?

WEEK 40

79. Reward Yourself

For a relatively small number of creative folk, enormous financial rewards are to be found in the marketplace. Some living painters command $5 million or $10 million a canvas at auction. Celebrity actors make millions of dollars per movie. A handful of writers earn multi-million dollar advances. A percentage of engineers invent processes that revolutionize industries and swell their bank accounts. Some biologists parlay their expertise and circumstances into six-figure biotech stock options. Who wouldn't want to join these exceptional few and make a fortune?

> They talk of the dignity of work. Bosh. The dignity is in the leisure.
>
> — HERMAN MELVILLE

Reaping financial reward for your creative work is a good thing. It allows you to maintain your car in running order, buy art supplies, and contribute to worthy causes. It makes it easier for your children to go to college and for your mate to retire when she wants to. You may well want to set your sights on financial rewards and do whatever it takes—studying the marketplace, fashioning personal contacts, aiming for technological breakthroughs—to better your odds of earning money from your creative efforts.

But making money can't be an everyday creative person's first or only priority. Her first priority is to manifest her creative potential in ways that feel deep and humane to her. She has a responsibility to herself to do ethical work, to help rather than harm her fellow human beings, and to add to, rather than subtract from, her culture. She also has the laudable desire to do creative work that is fascinating and personally meaningful, not dull and formulaic. For these reasons—and because the odds are long anyway that she'll be remunerated for her efforts—she will need to find other rewards, most of which she bestows on herself, that maintain her spirits and celebrate her accomplishments.

Today I went to the art store with one of my

daughters to buy her a traveling easel. There was nothing there that I needed, but still I spent four dollars on myself, just as a reward for working pretty well recently. I bought a tiny student art board, about two inches by three inches, which I will put up next to my computer and think of as an interesting all-white painting. I also purchased a plastic palette knife, because palette knives make me smile. From the 98¢ bin, I retrieved a tiny book on the history of lemons in art. I came away from the art store feeling happy and even rejuvenated.

> *If those who are the enemies of innocent amusements had the direction of the world, they would take away the spring.*
> — HONORÉ DE BALZAC

You could reward yourself by giving yourself an hour more each day to spend on your creative work. You could save up money and vacation time for a year and reward yourself with a week in Provence. You could save up for just a few days and reward yourself with some ripe peaches and plums. You could reward yourself with a visit to a museum or an evening at the opera. There are an infinite number of rewards you could bestow on yourself for working at your creative projects, and you deserve every one of them.

EXERCISE **79** • *Reward Yourself*

Take some time today and make a hefty list of rewards that you would enjoy receiving. Divide them into two columns: those that the world bestows on you and those that you can bestow on yourself. If you're hoping for the Nobel prize, a commission to design that new museum in Madrid, best-seller status for your next nonfiction book, or the services of a certain top theatrical agent, put that in the first column. If you'd like an outing in the country, new earrings, a subscription to a literary magazine, or fresh asparagus for dinner, put that in the second column.

Spend some time tomorrow thinking about how to get one of the rewards you listed in the first column. While the world must bestow it on you, there are still things you can do to increase your odds. If you put down "getting the theatrical agent Harry Jones to represent me," consider what you might do to woo Jones or to make yourself a more desirable commodity. You might send him Godiva chocolates when you send him your head shot and résumé. You might do a lot more auditioning than you've been doing recently. You might redouble your efforts to be hired for productions that he could be invited to attend. Make a plan to secure a reward from column one, then pledge to carry out your plan.

The day after tomorrow, reward yourself with something from column two. Subscribe to a literary magazine or buy some fresh asparagus. Thank yourself; and assure yourself that more rewards are coming.

WEEK 40

80. Stubbornly Keep Loving Yourself

It's hard to keep loving ourselves when we feel disappointed with our lack of effort, our lack of success in the marketplace, with the inadequacy of our ideas, with our troubled relationships, with the day job we maintain to make ends meet, with the many internal and external trials that devil us. If we aren't careful, these difficulties lead to self-hatred and acts of self-destructiveness. Not only does the novel we're trying to write sour on us; we sour on ourselves and start to behave in ways that kill our chances of writing that novel.

What will help you stubbornly keep loving yourself, given so many opportunities for self-hatred? First, it's vital to remember that you are not the same as your products. Even if you write a dozen short stories you don't like, you can—and should—continue to like yourself. Remind yourself that you can do deep work still; no past unrealized story has ruined your chances. The problem is not the stories in your drawer but the idea in your mind, that past failures are a predictor of future failures.

> *The earth remains jagged and broken to him or her who remains jagged and broken.*
> — WALT WHITMAN

In the same vein, it's important not to identify with some aspect of your personality. You are not the same as some attribute or quality you associate with yourself. Maybe you do procrastinate too much and maybe you do get too easily distracted when you sit down and try to compose. But it isn't wise to label yourself a "procrastinator" or "easily distractible." When you do this sort of self-labeling, the labels begin to stick and it becomes hard to think of yourself positively. Besides, they are simply false in their implication that you can't get to work sometimes and that you can't concentrate sometimes. You've done both a million times over. You will feel more self-love if you avoid pinning labels on yourself, especially labels like "untalented," "undisciplined," and "a failure."

The practice I've been describing is called "disidentification" in psychotherapy and "detachment training" in Zen Buddhism. Human beings are larger than and different from any of their attributes or accomplishments. It's always a mistake to identify with an attribute, whether positive or negative, or with a creative product, whether successful or unsuccessful. You are not your courage *or your* cowardice—you are a person who strives to be coura-geous but who is sometimes cow-ardly. You are not your good paintings *or* your bad paintings—you are a person who strives to paint well but who sometimes paints poorly. You are a *person* who grows, changes, and strives to do better and who has no good reason to limit herself by calling herself bad names.

> *We stumble and fall constantly, even when we are most enlightened.*
>
> — THOMAS MERTON

EXERCISE **80A** • *Make Some Messes, but Stubbornly Keep Loving Yourself*

For the next few days, you're going to make some messes.

This evening design and then start a mural on your bedroom wall, but paint it so ineptly that you really hate what you produce. (You can do this for real or just in your mind's eye.) Do a terrible job—but keep loving yourself.

Tomorrow evening pick up an instrument you've never played before, one, like the oboe, that even mas-ters have trouble playing. Produce some really rotten sounds. How far is *that* from music? But stubbornly keep loving yourself.

The day after tomorrow write something in-credibly banal. You can do it! But no matter how dull and lifeless your writing turns out, maintain self-compassion. Stubbornly keep loving yourself.

EXERCISE **80B** • *Get a Motto Engraved*

To aid in your efforts to stubbornly keep loving yourself, spend a little money and purchase a desk placard that you have engraved with some special motto that reminds you of your intention to love yourself always.

What phrase will you have engraved? "I am worth loving" is a resonant one. "The love starts here" is another possibility. The straightforward but eloquent "I love myself" is another. Create a list of phrases of this sort and select the one that feels the most appropriate and self-loving. Go to your local stationery store and have the placard fabricated. Display it proudly on your desk. Believe what it says.

PART 11

Work

Weeks 41-44

81. Wake Up Working

For the next four weeks—our last weeks of discussions and exercises—we'll focus on getting your creative work accomplished. I suggest that you then follow up these four weeks with two months of intense work on a creative project. That will round out our year together, a year during which you'll have made great strides toward becoming an everyday creative person. I hope you'll also have become a devotee of our religion, in which we worship truth, beauty, and goodness together.

Let's begin this week with the following question: when do creators create? Our first thought is that they create while sitting at their easel at noon or at their electron microscope late in the evening. Indeed, they do. But the more complete answer is that everyday creative people are engaged in the creative process all the time, as they do the dishes, stare into space, read the newspaper, or sleep. This is not news to you, but you may be unaware of just how much creating can and should go on away from your work space. In fact, that amount might be the lion's share, especially when you consider how valuable a time sleep is—maybe even *the* most valuable.

Everyday creative people go to bed thinking about their music, painting, writing, or scientific theories. They take to bed with them the musical problem that confounded them at four in the afternoon, so that their brain can solve it at night when worries about unpaid bills are forgotten for a while. The solution may not come that night or the next, but a brain so invited will come up with the solution eventually. You can't ask for more than that: to have a billion neuron elves working on your behalf while you, Santa, get your beauty rest.

What did you think about when you went to bed last night? If you're like most people, you probably stewed about the day's events, replayed an unpleasant conversation from work, or began dreading what tomorrow would bring. Maybe you lay there, restless and unable to sleep, listening to your lover snore. But there are far better things to do with that time than stew and worry. The very best thing is to ready yourself for a night's worth of creating.

> *A night of sleep is as much preparation for the subsequent day's activity as it is recovery from that of the previous day.*
> — J. ALLAN HOBSON

As soon as you crawl into bed, start thinking about your current creative project. Let's say it's a stage play. Murmur to yourself, "Now what exactly are Alice and Hannibal fighting about in Act Two?" Give your brain a real invitation to think. If you do, your brain will take sleep as its opportunity to make all the necessary connections. You'll drift off and sleep like a baby. When you wake up, you may feel compelled to head straight to the computer, so as to transcribe your characters' fight verbatim. One of the goals of an everyday creative person is to wake up this way every single day: to wake up working.

EXERCISE 81 • *Start to Sleep-Think and Wake Up Working*

Tonight, as you lie in bed, think about your current creative project. Ask yourself a question. It can be as general as "What does my painting need?" or as specific as "What will Sarah say when Anthony accuses her of sleepwalking?" Ask the question ever so gently. Let it be a real wonder ("Gosh, whatever will Sarah say?") and not a worry ("I've got to figure out what blasted words I'm going to put into Sarah's mouth!"). Drift off to sleep.

Sarah's response may startle you awake at three A.M. In that case, write it down and go back to bed.

> *Dream in a pragmatic way.*
> — ALDOUS HUXLEY

Maybe her response will wait until morning. In that case, write it down as soon as you wake up. Maybe it won't have arrived by morning. In any case, you need to set aside some work time first thing upon rising. If you go directly to work when you wake up, the answers to your creative questions, which may be *this close* to making themselves known, will have a chance to surface. If you start to use the night to sleep-think, you'll also want to begin each day in a new way, going straight to work as soon as you wake up, so as to make good use of your night efforts.

Can you go to bed in a different way tonight, with your creative project in mind? Can you go directly to work first thing tomorrow morning and see what fruits of your sleep-thinking may emerge? Do try. Sleep-thinking and waking up working are two of the best weapons in your creative arsenal.

82. Go Directly to Work

Not too long ago I got the following E-mail from a client, a poet and writing group facilitator who'd traveled to the Midwest to spend a month with some writer friends. She wrote:

Hi, Eric:

A friend of mine thought she would write a mystery the minute she retired. She retired, joined a writing group, but a year passed and still she hadn't done any work on the mystery. So she got stuck on the idea that she couldn't write it or else she would have written it already. I discussed your ideas with her and suggested that she work on writing first thing each morning, that she really hold the intention to write, and that whenever she had a thought about her book she should get right up and get to work on it. Now my friend has a great first chapter and she writes first thing each morning. And whenever she has a thought for the book, she's learned to stop everything and jot it down. So—as you know—it can be done!

> The best ideas come unexpectedly from a conversation or a common activity like watering the garden. These can get lost or slip away if not acted on when they occur.
>
> — RUTH ASAWA

People often have the desire to do creative work but can't make themselves go directly to their computer and write, to their studio to paint, or to their piano and compose. Something—some fear, some doubt, some memory of failure—paralyzes them and prevents them from taking that first step. If only they could take that first step, the second step and the third step would follow naturally and easily. But some invisible wall stands between them and their creative efforts. If they stood up and took one single step they'd crash through the block and be out the other side. But making that effort feels beyond them.

One way to prevent this block from happening is to use the phrase "I'm going directly to work" as a mantra and memory aid. "I'm going directly to work!" Can you feel the power in that phrase? The phrase is energizing, encouraging, even heroic-sounding. "I'm going directly to work!" To my ear, it sounds like your victory is assured. Do give it a try.

To delay is injustice.
— JEAN DE LA BRUYERE

Say it out loud right now. "I'm going directly to work!" Or just, "I'm going to work!" Or just, "Work!"

There are two senses to the phrase. One has to do with going to work as soon as an idea strikes you. The whole phrase might be "I'm going directly to work whenever an idea strikes me!" You conjure up the first line of a poem or you have the sudden insight that black is a warm color; either you go directly to work, starting that poem or a painting investigating black's warmth, or you don't. If you don't, the odds are pretty high that you'll lose the idea or feeling and miss an excellent opportunity to create. If you do, the chances are great that you'll be catapulted in a worthwhile direction and that you'll capture something important.

Some ideas keep returning and we really aren't in danger of losing them. But even with recurrent ideas, not taking action in the moment postpones—perhaps indefinitely—the creative encounter. With ideas and feelings that never return, if the one and only time they arrive we fail to go directly to work, we've lost them forever. Besides, how do we know which are which, the ones that will return and the ones that won't? Our wisest course is to go directly to work *every* time an idea that feels important strikes us.

The second sense of the phrase has to do with self-scheduling. It sounds like "I'm going directly to work at the time that I said I would!" You may or may not have any particular inspiration, but it's seven P.M., the hour you told yourself you were going to the computer to write. Either you go there punctually, as you promised yourself you would, or you don't. "Go directly to work" means both things: that when an idea strikes, you drop everything; and that when your work bell tolls, you answer it.

EXERCISE **82** • *Go Directly to Work.*

Get up right now. Go directly to your creative work.

Don't feel like it? Try anyway. Need a cup of coffee first? Skip it. Have a good reason not to work? Of course you do. Not sure of what you're working on? Figure it out as you work! Don't put off working by going to the bathroom, changing into more comfortable clothes, or making a few phones calls. Don't continue reading! Get up. Go to work. *Right now.*

WEEK 42

83. Really Sweat

In an earlier section, I asked you to exhaust yourself in the service of your creative work. Here, as we near the end of our time together, I want to repeat that working hard is an excellent thing. But your goal is to work hard *on* the work, not on brooding *about* the work. If, because of anxiety and self-doubt, you procrastinate and only think about working, you'll feel more exhausted than if you'd created for hours.

The students I teach are working adults with lots to do. They work sixty hours a week and then volunteer to do things like coach soccer. They aren't afraid to sweat. But, confronted by having to produce their first essay for me, which I assure them will take them a minimum of twenty hours to write, many try to squeeze it out at the last minute in a couple of hours. That never works.

It wasn't that they hadn't sweated enough. They'd sweated their full twenty hours' worth and more. But it was the wrong kind of sweating. They'd sweated worrying about the work instead of writing it. They'd squandered buckets of adrenaline on not starting. You can sweat by not sculpting or you can pick up your chisel. You can sweat by not practicing or you can pick up your clarinet. There's good sweat and there's bad sweat. Which do you want to secrete?

> The strong do not hesitate. They settle down, they sweat, they go on to the end. They exhaust the ink, they use up the paper.
>
> — JULES RENARD

EXERCISE 83 • *Really Sweat*

Get a towel ready. Take several days off from work, or schedule some long blocks of time for yourself every evening for several days running. Over these next several days, you're going to write a short story. (If you prefer to engage in your own creative work, reframe this exercise. You could write several songs, begin to learn a new musical repertoire, etc. But I think you'll find it valuable to try this exercise exactly the way it's framed.)

EXERCISE 83A • *This Exercise Will Develop Your Courage*

Pick an idea: say, to write about your sister's rape. Phone a friend and say, "I'm starting a story about my sister's rape, and I want you to call me up tomorrow to see how it's going." When the phone rings tomorrow, answer it. Say, "I'm writing right now and I'll talk to you later" or "I'm starting as soon as we hang up." Ask your friend to call you up every day this week, even if you don't like the idea of being monitored and even if the sound of the phone ringing begins to feel like a reproach or a bomb exploding.

EXERCISE **83B** • *This Exercise Will Develop Your Judgment*

Take your story idea and imagine it differently. Change the events of the rape, moving it from midnight to noon, from the city to the suburbs. Change the assailant and change the victim. See how this new story feels. Does it capture something even more important? Or was the original idea better? Remember, your friend will be calling. Feel the pressure but keep your mind clear (remember, you can be calm and anxious simultaneously). Commit to one version of the story, but not before you give the alternatives their due.

EXERCISE **83C** • *This Exercise Will Develop Your Critical Thinking Skills*

Analyze your budding story. Tear it into its constituent parts: the part that's about fear, the part that's about bad luck, the part that's about inevitability. What is at the very heart? Concentrate on that. Select a word or phrase—like "paralyzing fear"—that stands for the story's center, then write it in the margin next to every paragraph. Gauge to what extent each paragraph supports that quality.

EXERCISE **83D** • *This Exercise Will Develop Your Creative Muscles*

Write your story. Then rewrite it. Then rewrite again, if it needs further revision. Write late into the night for as many consecutive nights as needed.

EXERCISE **83E** • *This Exercise Will Develop Your Dexterity*

Begin a second story in this "series." For instance, you might write about the rape from the point of view of your victim's mother, who has no idea what's going on across town at that very moment. You might write it from the point of view of a policeman who arrives at the scene or from the point of view of God, who let this happen. Spend some real time sweating over this second story of yours— and if you're willing, even take it to completion.

> *I felt that the only way I could work properly was by using the absolute maximum of observation and concentration that I could possibly muster.*
>
> — LUCIAN FREUD

When your week is up, congratulate yourself. Hit the shower.

WEEK 42

84. Make Plans and Schedules

It's good to have a plan to follow for your creative efforts. Your plan might sound like the following: "I want to return to nature for my painting inspiration and get more of my feelings about the mystery of life into my art"; or "I want to write a mystery series set in different parts of London. I'd like to set the first one in Hampstead and have Hampstead Heath play a large part, so that readers are reminded of Sherlock Holmes and *The Hound of the Baskervilles*"; or "I mean to devote the next three years to the study of the Hmong in the central valley of California. It fascinates me how this culture, which kept its traditions first in China and then in Vietnam through every sort of adversity for a thousand years, should have lost them so quickly after just thirty years of the American experience."

> *At sixty-three years of age, less a quarter, one still has plans.*
> — COLETTE

In order to create your plan, you will need to think about what you mean to work on and what you hope to accomplish. Then you'll want to articulate the steps of your plan and the actions you intend to take to bring your plan to fruition. The central task here is to go deep, so that you choose a project that is rich and right for you. Once you can feel in a visceral way that you've chosen well, articulating your plan is little more than drafting a clear sentence or two that captures the essence of your thoughts.

Then you add a few sentences about the steps required to turn your plan into reality. These steps might include: researching the history of the Hmong, interviewing several Hmong families in the Modesto and Merced areas, and studying a particular Hmong-on-Hmong crime that reflects the intergenerational conflict that particularly interests you.

Your next task is to make a schedule. To begin with, you might just schedule the first week: say, to spend two hours a day on Tuesday, Wednesday, and Thursday thinking about the plot of your Hampstead mystery, a few hours on Saturday at the library or on the Internet researching Hampstead Heath, and half a day on Sunday writing a biography of your detective, in order to get acquainted with her. For a while, you might continue making such week-by-week schedules. Then, once you've acquired a better picture of the project—and know that the book needs to be, say, 80,000 words in length, and that you typically produce about 500 words during each writing stint—you'd make a schedule to complete the first draft of the mystery, mapping out your next eight or ten months of work.

> *If I don't paint for a single day, I don't feel well physically or mentally.*
>
> — RAPHAEL SOYER

You can keep to your plan by beginning each day with the self-reminder that you're working on this project and by affirming that you have goals to meet and a schedule to keep. Probably you'll have to modify both your plan and your schedule over time. Your schedule might change if you have to work longer hours at your day job or because you discover that your novel needs to be 10,000 words longer than you anticipated. Your plan would change if you realized that you wanted to focus on a certain Hmong youth gang rather than on Hmong culture in general, or that now you wanted to make a documentary film rather than the nonfiction book you'd been planning. Make these necessary changes; then keep to your new plan and your new schedule.

You can't plan in advance for everything—every mood swing, every mistake you might make in execution, every shift in your circumstances. But you can keep updating your plan and you can demand of yourself that you always have an up-to-date plan in place. You can get into the habit of making schedules for your creative life and then following them. Acquiring these habits will help you maintain focus on your creative life and will dramatically increase both your productivity and your happiness.

EXERCISE 84 • *Make a Plan and a Schedule*

Over the next few days, take pen to paper and begin to articulate a current, up-to-date plan for your creative life. Meditate on the question of what creative project would really engage you and challenge you. Once your plan comes into focus, work out the steps required to turn your dream into reality and schedule at least one week of work in support of your new project.

If you currently have a plan and a schedule in place, take some time during the next few days to revisit them. Since you want to revisit them periodically anyway, to make sure they're still on target, take this period as that opportunity.

WEEK 43

85. Be Patient but Not Idle

A time will come when your creative products will be out in the world, making their rounds. You'll be waiting to hear if you got the role in that play you auditioned for and are dying to appear in. You'll be anxiously hoping to hear from the editor who said that she liked your nonfiction book proposal and was now "taking it to meetings." If you create you will also wait, and while you're waiting you will want to be patient but not idle.

You need patience, because responses from the world often take a long time. What you've created may not be good enough or may not have commercial appeal and what you may receive back after your long wait is a rejection. But even if your work is good enough and even if it's ultimately wanted, connecting with the right consumer or having your ideas accepted in the intellectual marketplace can be a long, drawn-out affair. I've sold a dozen books to medium and large publishers in the last decade, but I sold nothing to sizable publishers for the fifteen years before that, even though some of the manuscripts were, I believe, worthy. Many creative people have the same story to tell. Patience is not only a virtue, it's a necessity.

> *I go to my studio every day. Some days the work comes easily. Other days nothing happens. Yet on the good days the inspiration is only an accumulation of all the other days, the nonproductive ones.*
>
> — BEVERLY PEPPER

A writer friend of mine, who hasn't been published yet but whose latest proposal is being looked at by an editor at a large publishing house, asked me how it could be taking so long to get a response. Six months had passed already! My reply was, "Easy." Here's how it takes six months. Week one: editor Dan brings two new proposals to the weekly editorial meeting, neither of which is yours. Week two: Dan again brings two proposals to the meeting, one of which is yours, but he only gets to present one, and he chooses to present the other one. Week three: the meeting is taken up with all sorts of business and no new proposals have the chance to come forward. Week four: other editors go first and there is no time for Dan to present your book. Week five: Dan brings up your book. There is some interest, but people wonder what the competition looks like. Dan asks Scott, his assistant, to visit the local Borders and Barnes & Noble stores to size up the competition.

Weeks six and seven: because Scott hasn't found the time yet to get to the bookstore, Dan can't move forward with your proposal.

Let me cut this short and not detail the next twenty weeks that your proposal will spend at this publishing house, as one thing after another comes up to delay a decision. Suffice it to say that no one is ill-disposed toward your book, nor is anyone acting unprofessionally or unethically. It is simply that there are too many competing projects and too much going on. Your book has not leaped over these natural obstacles—which it would if you were famous or if your book had tremendous sales potential—and hopped onto the fast track. It is moving as proposals often do, from the writer's point of view at a snail's pace.

> *If you devote yourself to your art, much evil is avoided that would happen otherwise if you were idle.*
>
> — ALBRECHT DÜRER

You will need patience to survive this. But while you're waiting for your products to be purchased, you also want to keep producing. As an everyday creative person, you will disappoint yourself if you say, "I won't start my next screenplay until this one sells." You may have a great emotional investment in that screenplay and great hopes for it, but you also have love and energy to devote to your next one. Remind yourself of the value of detaching from work that's out of your hands and committing to new work that wants to be born.

EXERCISE **85A** • *Practice Patience*

For the next few days, practice patience as you go about your routine business. See if you can consciously make your morning commute or your wait for the bus more bearable by saying to yourself, "I can be patient." Make note of how good it feels and how much anxiety you release when, as you wait on a slow-moving checkout line at the supermarket, you switch your inner language from "What's taking so long?" to "Maybe I'll scribble a few notes for my novel." Dream up and try out a variety of patience-building techniques and strategies.

EXERCISE **85B** • *Dispute Idleness*

Buy a calendar that you keep for the purpose of noting how many days go by between periods of creative effort. Choose the maximum number of days you're willing to let slip by without creating—say, one or two. If it happens that you painted on Tuesday but not on Wednesday or Thursday, then first thing Friday morning go directly to your studio.

WEEK 43

86. Become Water

Many of us stubbornly live rectangularly, bound on all four sides by restrictions we ourselves invent. To the east, we bind ourselves with the laws of conformity. To the west, we bind ourselves by denying our talents. To the north, we bind ourselves by claiming to be too busy. To the south, we bind ourselves with our doubts and insecurities. By whatever masons these walls were built initially, we now maintain them ourselves. We have an idea and run with it straight to a wall: "This idea is way too big for me!" We encounter a gorgeous natural effect—a thin streak of heartbreaking violet in a thunderstorm sky—and refuse to retain it: "Who has time for that?" We feel a tale growing in us and we stop it violently: "Don't you come here! I'll just ruin you!" We are our own best jailers.

Yes, it would be good to smash these prison walls to smithereens. But here's another idea. Become water and flow right over, through, and around them. Become water and flow over the highest dams, the ones you've built to restrict yourself. Flood the whole plain with your creativity. If you don't know what I mean, imagine turning on the water in your bathtub and stopping up the drain. Where does the water go? Everywhere. It climbs, it seeps, it gushes, it meanders. Become like the leading edge of that water—become someone who flows down stairs, flows around corners, effortlessly bypasses chair legs and ottomans.

You've had the following experience countless times. One moment you couldn't seem to do something—start a school paper, solve a problem, ready a presentation. The very next moment you could. What happened? Well, where there was rock there became water. You relaxed and flowed. This is the real definition of surrender, a word that's hard to fathom. We are usually like rock, jagged and self-defeating, adamant in our refusal to do what we want to do, hard as nails, as well-defended as a stone fortress. Then some invisible switch gets thrown and we surrender. Like water, we glide right where we want to go. Something inside of us—the brave part, the smart part, the good part, the loving part, the life-affirming part, the optimistic part, the sure part—wins the day and melts our icecap. We flow again.

"Flow" has become a popular word. The psychologist Mihaly Csikszentmihalyi uses it to stand for that optimal state of being that I've called in previous books "the trance of working." Susan Perry, in her book *Writing in Flow,* reports on her interviews with seventy-five well-known writers, who discuss what "flow" means to them and the tricks they've learned to achieve that state. Jon Kabat-Zinn, author of *Wherever You Go There You Are,* relates flow to the Buddhist idea of non-doing: "Non-doing simply means letting things be and allowing them to unfold in their own way. Enormous effort can be involved, but it is a graceful, knowledgeable, effortless effort, a 'doerless doing,' cultivated over a lifetime." When you enter this state—when you flow like water—you bring all of your talents and resources to your creative work.

> There were times when depression, anxiety, whatever, would keep me from writing. I still get depressed and anxious, but I just don't let it stop me. I've just learned to move it to one side if I want to work.
>
> — DAVID ST. JOHN

Learn what facilitates this process in you. Some people need to have their desks clean: only then can they flow. Others need to have their cat nearby or a cup of coffee handy. Some need to reply to all of their E-mail before they can even think about flowing. Others need to quiet their mind or remind themselves that they have permission to create. Some need to make an effort to let go of recent disappointments. What do you need? What works for you?

EXERCISE 86 • *Become Water*

Flow from where you're sitting, reading this book, right over to your work space.

Flow around every obstacle you encounter, including any you've erected yourself. If a blocking idea arises—that this exercise is stupid, that you don't know what to work on, that your work space is a mess, that you're too tired to create, that you don't know how to flow—flow right around it. Feel like flowing water. Seep beneath a block or through the tiniest crack in an obstructing wall. There is nothing you need to do but flow. No willpower is needed. No effort is required. All you need is a movement like water flowing or like some sinuous dance, a movement that is all ease and effortlessness.

> *What I'm after is that state of concentration in which everything flows to and from the work. Then, when I walk into my study, I bring this kind of energy with me, readying me to focus inward.*
>
> — ANDREA HOLLANDER BUDY

Stop reading this book. Flow over to your current creative project and work for an hour.

WEEK 44

87. Pick Yourself Up

When an actress is informed at an audition that she can't act a lick, what must she do? Pick herself up. When a pianist botches a performance, what must he do? Pick himself up. When a botanist tries out a new method of crossbreeding that ultimately fails to work, what must she do? Pick herself up. When a chef prepares brilliant Spanish dishes but his restaurant fails, what must he do? Pick himself up.

The metaphor of a religion of creativity can help. If you remind yourself that you have the desire to create, that creating is a worthy enterprise, that meaning and good spirits return when you create, that others may be moved or helped by what you create, that, in short, you are a disciple of a religion whose principles, practices, and purposes you find valuable, you may find the motivation to pick yourself up.

How do you pick yourself up if you've been dealt a powerful blow or if you feel particularly stuck and blue? The answer has three parts. First, you mustn't give up hope. If you're depressed, that means that you're feeling hopeless, so it might seem as if the horse has left the corral already. But even if you're severely depressed, it's still likely that hope is waiting in the wings. Countless suicidal people have come back from the edge. Even some monumentally depressed creative folks have found the wherewithal to continue—van Gogh didn't, but Beethoven did; Virginia Woolf didn't, but Tolstoy did; Hemingway didn't, but Georgia O'Keeffe did. Hope springs eternal in most of us.

> *The attacks of which I have been the object have broken the spring of life in me. People don't realize what it feels like to be constantly insulted.*
>
> — EDOUARD MANET

Second, you need to rearrange your inner reality, letting go of pain, hurt, anger, disappointment and the thoughts and feelings that deplete and stymie you. In their place, you want to fill up with love, purpose, passion, and other qualities that animate you, as quickly as you can but as slowly as you must. The techniques for letting go and filling up are as old as Zen and as new as cognitive therapy; they boil down to monitoring your thoughts and substituting positive ones for the negative ones. You can call this process "detachment training," "thought substitution," or affirming yourself.

Third, you need to rearrange your outer reality, doing whatever is necessary to improve your circumstances and change the facts that contribute to your pain and sadness. If you are not in love and want love, that requires work and a presence in the world. If your career as a singer, biologist, or novelist is stalled, the steps to unstalling will involve both inner work and outer work. If you feel alienated, you'll need to connect with others; if you feel unheard, you'll need to entice an audience; if you feel uninspired, you'll need to seek inspiration from the world

> *It was always disappointing to see that what I could really master in terms of form boiled down to so little.*
> — ALBERTO GIACOMETTI

and from your own imagination. Rekindling hope, engaging in inner work, and venturing into the world amount to a complete plan for picking yourself up when you're down.

EXERCISE **87** • *Plan for Pick-Me-Ups*

There will come a time when you'll need to pick yourself up and find your way back to your creative life. On certain days, you'll lose your sense of purpose or your ability to cope. Now is the time to plan for such moments. Choose items from the following list that have worked for you before or that you think might work for you in the future and personalize them by writing out how you would put them into practice. For example, if you choose "talk to someone," name the person you'd seek out and think about what benefits a conversation with him or her would afford you.

- surrender to the feeling
- improve your self-talk
- do something you love
- ask for help
- remember a success
- put on healing music
- express your feelings
- seek out a friend
- detach from your ego
- make amends

- reward yourself
- talk to someone
- examine your past
- live in the moment
- visualize a better future
- make yourself create
- be of service
- pray to the universe
- turn outward

- dance your rage
- sing a lullaby
- join with others for support
- monitor your thoughts
- go on a retreat
- find healing advice
- satisfy a need
- consciously choose hope
- turn inward

WEEK 44

88. Simply Create

A friend of mine, a psychotherapist and dharma teacher in a Korean branch of Zen Buddhism, describes Zen as a lens through which he sees reality. Everything about the world is filtered through his understanding of the principles and practices of Zen. When he sits down to eat, he eats in a Zen way, enjoying his food and keeping the television off. When he counsels clients, he counsels them in a Zen way, beginning sessions with sitting meditation. For him, everything is simply Zen.

That's the way of everyday creative people, too. We see everything through the lens of creativity. We define creativity as manifesting our potential, and we go about manifesting it. We define creativity as using our brains, and we endeavor to do that. We define creativity as having heart, and so we feel deeply. We associate our creativity with a love of justice, a passion for freedom, and compassion for our brothers and sisters, so we are staunch in defense of life's best principles. We produce: sonnets, sculptures, herb gardens, vaccines, exposés, independent films, earthquake detectors, performance pieces. All of this taken together is our life: our life as simple creators.

When you see everything through the lens of creativity, when you live life as an everyday creative person, you create as a matter of course. Creating becomes the most natural thing in the world, as natural as breathing. If a problem arises at work, you attempt to solve it creatively—and usually you do. When you want to cook a special meal, you have a functioning imagination available that presents you with menu ideas full of sparkle and wit. When you have a thank-you note to write, you write a beautiful one. When you have an empty bedroom wall to fill, you make something to fill it. When an evil occurs, you fight it.

> *Art! What a concept! It saved my life! A place where you can do as you please!*
> — WILLIAM WILEY

Even though an everyday creative person creates as a matter of course, it is unlikely that she will live happily ever after. She takes on too much of the world's suffering, engages in too many battles for the sake of truth, beauty, and goodness, and repeatedly attempts deep work that is taxing and even exhausting. Yet she is sometimes happier than anyone else. Every so often she produces excellent work that fills her with pride and satisfaction. Every so often she reflects that she is living her life consciously and responsibly, which makes her happy. In the religion of creativity, there are many potential and actual happinesses available.

But I don't want to minimize the difficulties that everyday creative people face. I've been writing about creativity for more than fifteen years and I've examined these difficulties in book after book. In this book, too, I've addressed chronic depression, heartbreaking envy, work blocks, relationship failures, harsh marketplace realities, and many of the other problems that confront everyday creative people on a regular basis. But there is always the question: would a person with a good mind and a large heart have been better off not opting for our religion? Probably not. Would she have lived a happier life and felt more fulfilled doing work that paid well but that she didn't believe in? Unlikely. In short, it's possible that this person was doomed to suffer by virtue of the fact that she was born fully human. Maybe opting for creativity didn't worsen her prospects but actually afforded her a measure of comfort.

> *I hope with all my heart that there will be painting in heaven.*
>
> — JEAN-BAPTISTE-CAMILLE COROT

I think it's possible that if you have a brain demanding to be used, beautiful dreams to realize, and other attributes that mark you as a potential disciple of our religion, you might as well join us and live your life as a creative person. What do you think?

EXERCISE **88** • *Simply Create*

If you follow the plan of this book, next week you'll begin two months of work on a creative project. I'd like you to spend the rest of this week preparing for that adventure by letting go, as best you can, of the inner strictures and impediments that stand between you and creating deeply. To accomplish that, review some earlier exercises and refresh your memory about forgiving yourself, exorcising inner demons, and so on, with an eye to readying yourself for your upcoming adventure.

As a preparatory step, take this opportunity to write down your answer to an updated version of the question I posed in week one: what obstacles still stand between you and your own creativity? Try to name any remaining blocks; then, using what you've learned this year, craft a plan to overcome them. Finally, grow joyful as you contemplate your coming months of creating!

Create

Weeks 45-52

89. Work on Your Creative Project

I hope you've found these last ten months enlightening and transformative and that you've taken the opportunity to start and really work on a significant creative project.

For the next two months, devote yourself to that creative project or to one that you start now. You have all the tools you need: you've carved out a work space for yourself, you've practiced making time for your creative efforts, you know what to do when a bout of the blues hits, you're more adept at telling the truth and at lavishing love on yourself and on your work. If an obstacle arises, look back over the exercises in this book. You'll find just the right one to help you break through a block or recover your motivational juices.

Two months is a long time. You could write a draft of a novel, even just working evenings. You could learn a pottery technique like raku and produce some fine pieces. You could conceive an idea for a full-length documentary film, prepare your budget, and begin to seek financing. You could design and activate your business website. You could prepare a workshop on a subject you know well and make arrangements to teach it. You could do a lot.

The religion of creativity is only a metaphor, but even as mere metaphor it can lift your spirits and remind you how you want to live your life. An "everyday creative person" is another metaphor with roots that run deep. It is enormously satisfying to approach whatever life has to offer in a creative way and equally joyful to take your thoughts and feelings about life and transform them into worthy things like vaccines, novels, and songs. When asked to summarize what constituted a mentally healthy life, Freud replied "To love and to work." In our religion, we amend that only slightly: our goals are to love and to create.

In a world that has ceased to believe in sin, the artist is responsible for the preaching.

— ALBERT CAMUS

I mentioned earlier that while writing this book I've also been writing a book called *Sleep Thinking*. In fact, I've never found it possible to write two books at once, and I'm not so much writing *Sleep Thinking* as jotting down occasional notes about it. But that book is growing quite nicely because I've hired my eldest daughter, Natalya, to research it. She finished high school this June and is spending the two-month period before beginning college in my employ. As you can imagine, the summer between high school and college can be a hard one, but she is negotiating it well because she is creating.

As I watch her bringing back stacks of books from the library or getting up early in the morning to jot down ideas, I am happy for the help I'm receiving but ecstatic that she is an everyday creative person. When she comes to me with an anecdote or quote she's discovered or an idea that's occurred to her, I'm pleased for the sake of the book but overjoyed that she is a practicing member of the religion of creativity. It will sound sentimental but still I need to say it: it makes me want to cry.

We human beings possess talents, skills, and qualities that are only exercised when we create. We do our best job of making and maintaining personal meaning when we create. Whether you're a physician, physicist, sculptor, dancer, carpenter, or poet, you can choose to live each day in a creative way, manifesting your potential and launching into ambitious creative projects. It may take you some time to find the creative outlet you really love, but once you discover it, you will always have a spiritual home to which to return. It may require a very long period of trial and error before you begin to do excellent creative work, but when you finally accomplish that work, you will feel proud and happy.

We have no art, we do everything as well as we can.

— BALINESE PROVERB

Since I am calling creativity a religion, let me end with a prayer. I pray that you find a creative outlet that you love, enjoy it for a lifetime, and do creative work that is good, beautiful, and true. I pray that you couple your creative efforts with the other elements of a life worth living: intimate relating and compassionate action in the world. Let us determine to support each other in this religion of ours, even if we never meet. Life is too short not to create, not to love, and not to lend a helping hand to our brothers and sisters.

Getting in Touch

I hope that you will take the opportunity to get in touch with me and share your thoughts about this book and your experiences as a creative person.

My E-mail address is: amaisel@sirius.com

My message machine phone number is: (925) 689-0210

My fax number is: (925) 689-0210

My mailing address is:

Eric Maisel, ph.d.
P.O. Box 613
Concord, CA 94522-0613

You may also want to visit my website: www.ericmaisel.com
Thank you!